the **GOOD,**
the **BAD,** and the
FURRY

Library of Congress Cataloging in Publication Number: 2004112081

ISBN 1-59474-021-6

Printed in Singapore

Typeset in Bell MT and Gill Sans
Design and Iconography by Karen Onorato
Illustrations by David Merrell

Distributed in North America by Chronicle Books
85 Second Street
San Francisco, CA 94105

10 9 8 7 6 5 4 3 2 1

Quirk Books
215 Church Street
Philadelphia, PA 19106
www.quirkbooks.com

the GOOD,
the BAD, and the
FURRY

choosing the dog that's right for you

by Sam Stall

Foreword by Edwin J. Sayres,
President of the American Society for the
Prevention of Cruelty to Animals

QUIRK BOOKS

PHILADELPHIA

Contents

Appendix

Acknowledgments 208

Foreword

When I was asked to write the foreword to *The Good, the Bad, and the Furry*, I was flattered—and a little hesitant. As the current president of the American Society for the Prevention of Cruelty to Animals (ASPCA), and the former president of the San Francisco Society for the Prevention of Cruelty to Animals (SFSPCA), I've spent a good part of my adult life working around abandoned, abused, and just generally unwanted dogs. Many of these unfortunate animals have fallen into the non-purebred, or "mutt," category, and places like the ASPCA and the SFSPCA are often viewed by the general public as little more than repositories for "second-rate" dogs. But this is simply not the case, and I firmly believe that the book you're holding right now is an important work that will go a long way toward dispelling this notion.

Why? Because the book recognizes one important fact: Animal cruelty—whether it consists of outright abuse, benign neglect, or simply frustrated abandonment—begins and ends with people. There's no way around it. Dogs are dogs, whether they're born with perfect bloodlines under the watchful eye of an outstanding breeder, or anonymously in the basement of an abandoned tenement. The behavior of a breed dog may be easier to predict, but that's about as far as it goes. Once a dog—whatever its lineage—is placed in the care of an uninformed, or unprepared, or even actually cruel human being, all bets are off. Even if the dog is not physically hurt, it will at best spend most of its days trying to gauge its unhappy owner's intentions, or at worst, sitting back in a cage at a local shelter, unable to understand what it has done to deserve abandonment, leaving the animal that much more insecure about what will happen when someone else decides to shower it with love—for a while.

If you're contemplating the adoption or purchase of a dog—purebred or otherwise—or if you've already adopted or purchased a dog and would like to know more about the animal you've decided to make a part of your life, I urge you to read this book. The problem of homeless companion animals in this country is a huge one, and it will only be alleviated when current and potential adopters arm themselves with the right kind of information about their dogs—and when they decide to make a serious, honest assessment of the type of human/animal relationship they're looking for, and the kind of commitment that they're willing to make.

Edwin J. Sayres
President
The American Society for the Prevention of Cruelty to Animals

Oh great, another breed guide.

If there's one thing the world doesn't need (besides more boy bands), it's one more fat book listing the vital statistics of the planet's roughly 500 dog varieties. Go to any bookstore and you'll find rows of these tomes, lined up like ticks on a German shepherd's back, each one poised to explain why everything from the Labrador retriever to the redbone coonhound is just the right pet for you.

But statistics show that not every dog is right for every person. In fact, some dogs aren't right for most people. That doesn't mean such breeds aren't fit for human companionship. It just means they require owners who understand their special needs and are willing to accommodate them. Unfortunately, lots of people purchase the wrong pooch, for the wrong reasons. For proof, look no further than your nearest city pound or animal shelter. Millions of perfectly good canines—including armies of purebreds—land in these places each year, dumped like a two-year-old SUV with an expired lease. Their only "fault" is that they weren't what their owners anticipated them to be.

So why didn't they do what their owners expected? Because in many cases their owners didn't *know* what to expect. Perhaps they purchased a basset hound because they liked its looks, not realizing that these dogs drool profusely and are very hard to house-train. Or maybe they acquired a Weimaraner because they heard it was a "good family dog," only to discover that they can shed like mad, follow you around like a stalker, and tear the house apart if left alone too long.

None of which is the dog's fault. It's never the dog's fault. They are simply doing what they were designed to do. It's the owner's fault for not learning about the chosen breed's characteristics in advance.

Unfortunately, discovering the truth isn't as easy as it should be. More than a few books and Web pages wax poetic about various dogs' Frisbee-catching abilities and show-ring stats. But sometimes you have to do a great deal of digging to unearth all the slobbering, urine-soaked, yard-destroying details of life with particular breeds.

That's where this guide comes in. Its object isn't to be diplomatic or to show every dog in the best possible light. It just lays out the nitty-gritty details—the good, the bad, and the furry—pertaining to more than 100 different varieties. Because if more people knew the facts, those facts might dissuade some of them from buying the wrong canines for the wrong reasons—and then discarding them like last year's fashions.

That would be a very good thing, because the world is filled with homeless dogs tossed aside by people who lacked just this sort of information. Consider the case of Mellie, the tiny bichon frise who, after spending most of its first four months of life imprisoned inside a dog crate by a neglectful owner, was finally fobbed off on a volunteer for a breed rescue service. The volunteer learned that the poor animal (whose full name is Magnolia's Melanie of Special Times) was the daughter of a Westminster Dog Show Best in Show Grand Champion, which is as close as one gets to canine royalty.

That sort of thing happens a lot, as any breed rescue worker can confirm. And because they know all about the problems that can get particular dog varieties in trouble, we've drawn on the experiences of rescue workers nationwide to flesh out this book's dozens of canine profiles. When it comes to dog-related hassles, they've heard it all—and they're more than willing to tell all, if it keeps their beloved breeds out of the clutches of people ill-equipped to cope with the dogs' various foibles.

Which brings us to the most important factor in any decision to buy a dog—you. A potential buyer needs, first and foremost, to assess his or her own habits and outlook before worrying about those of a potential canine companion. Are you a neat freak? Do you prize your free time and want nothing to interfere with it? Do you travel a lot? Then do the dog world a huge favor and get a goldfish instead of a canine.

If all you want is a status symbol, a furry fashion accessory, or a nanny for your kids, a dog isn't for you. But if you seek a loyal friend and devoted companion, you've come to the right place.

In order to be a successful dog owner, you must see your canine not as an object, but as a buddy. Because if a dog is your friend, suddenly all the things that can make owning one seem intolerable *become* tolerable. To someone who truly loves dogs, having a Weimaraner up their butt 24/7 isn't a problem. And if you truly love your basset hound, you don't fret about the drool stringers flung on your furniture, walls, and ceilings. We all have friends we love so much that we are willing to overlook behavior from them that we'd never tolerate from strangers. Well, a dog should—indeed, must—be just that sort of friend.

A dedicated dog owner understands that wiping up slobber is a small price to pay for what he or she gets in return. As anyone who has ever loved one already knows, a dog always, always, gives more than it gets. In exchange for food, shelter, guidance, and a little forbearance, a dog offers the sort of unquestioning devotion that the average person seldom, if ever, receives from fellow humans.

Of course, you know you're unworthy of such devotion. We're all unworthy. And yet, there it is, tail wagging, staring up at you from the hair-covered living room couch—a living creature that thinks you're Gandhi and Mother Teresa and Martin Luther King, all wrapped up in one. Remember that. And don't let your dog down.

The Top Five Worst Reasons to Get a Dog

1 I saw it in the pet-store window and I fell in love. Adopting a dog is not a spur-of-the-moment decision. You need to learn about the particular breed and whether it is compatible with your lifestyle. Then you have to find a healthy, well-socialized, responsibly bred representative of that breed—something a pet-store puppy almost certainly is not.

2 I saw a particular breed in a movie/TV show/commercial and just had to have it. Whenever a breed gets a lot of high-profile exposure (the Dalmatian in *101 Dalmatians*; the Brussels griffon in *As Good as It Gets*; the Jack Russell terrier on *Frasier*), the same sad cycle repeats itself. First, the dog becomes wildly popular as lots of people rush to acquire it; and second, usually within six months, animal shelters fill up with that particular animal as its owners lose interest and discard it.

3 I need something to shore up my manhood. Imagine you're a low-level drone at your job, a 120-pound weakling, a goofball who no one takes seriously, or all of the above. Getting a big, scary dog will not change this. It will only make you a weakling with a big, scary dog—a dog that you probably won't be able to manage any more effectively than your personal or professional lives.

4 Puppies are cute! Yes, they are. Trouble is, they grow up to become adult dogs. So before you start mooning over that baby Newfoundland, you might want to read up on just how big Junior will become.

5 I want to get it for my kids, so they can learn about responsibility. No matter how many lectures you give about how they need to feed/water/walk the dog, the final responsibility will always be yours. A canine is not a teaching tool—unless you want to teach a young child that pulling on the ears or tail of a dog is an excellent way to get bitten. The best way to teach responsibility is to provide a good example by taking good care of your dog.

The Story of Man's Best Friend
and How He Came to Be That Way

Dog breeds can look startlingly different, and individual dogs possess distinct personalities. But all, from the grubbiest mutt to the prissiest purebred, hold certain mental traits in common—traits inherited from their genetic forebears, the wolves. Wolves know how to stalk game, chase it, and kill it. And most importantly, they know how to multiply their effectiveness by working and living together in a community—the pack.

Humans exploited these behaviors to turn the wolf/dog (hereafter referred to as the "dog") into a useful companion. Canines could be taught to see clans of humans as their pack. They could help guard the camp, track prey, and increase the striking power of hunting parties, all in exchange for the less-desirable (from a human perspective) portions of the kill, a spot by the fire, and perhaps an occasional pat on the head.

But this was only the beginning of the dog's usefulness. As human societies grew more complex, they started tweaking the canine through selective breeding. This produced a menagerie that includes everything from present-day Pomeranians to pinschers. But it wasn't just, or even primarily, the dogs' bodies that got reworked. Their minds were messed with, too. Various parts of the old wolf behaviors were either deleted or developed, allowing dogs to take on tasks their wild ancestors never would have dreamed of doing.

Take sheepdogs. A canine that herds sheep is basically using its wolf-given ability to stalk and intimidate large groups of herbivores. But there's one key difference. While the "stalk the sheep" portion of its predator programming still functions superbly, the "kill the sheep" portion has, for obvious reasons, been suppressed. That's why a shepherd can leave his dog in charge of 100 sheep with every confidence that there will still be 100 when he returns.

Over the eons several broad categories of working dogs arose, differentiated primarily by the portions of their old wolf behaviors that were accentuated. They were designed to fight things (terriers excel at this), chase things (the greyhound), herd things (the Border collie), find things (the bloodhound), guard things (the Doberman pinscher), and haul things (the Siberian husky). Almost every dog breed, even the most unlikely, at one time performed some type of useful work. The tiny, monkey-faced affenpinscher was a rat catcher; the poodle was a hunting dog; and the short-legged corgi somehow managed to herd cattle.

These old professions still matter today, even if the only thing your corgi ever herds is the neighborhood children. The job a particular breed was originally designed to do determines in large part its outlook on life, its attitude toward you, and what it's like to live with. For instance, hounds such as the beagle and Afghan were designed to operate in front, sometimes way in front, of hunting parties. It was their job to pursue game over open country, corner it on their own initiative, and then wait for backup. Which means that the typical hound is an independent thinker, always ready to strike out on its own after a potential target—even if the "target" happens to be a squirrel or your neighbor's kid on a bike. Likewise terriers, bred to exterminate everything from rats to badgers, are convinced they were put on this earth to make life hell for woodland creatures. Training can sometimes lessen such behaviors, but nothing, absolutely nothing, can completely stop them. So when a greyhound takes off after a bird or a Jack Russell digs up a tulip bed, they aren't misbehaving. They're simply obeying instructions etched in their DNA.

No matter what breed you ultimately select, there's bound to be some aspect of its personality or behavior that drives you buggy. But while all breeds, and all individuals, display their own peculiar personality quirks and tics, one wolflike behavior cuts across all branches of the canine family tree. Your dog still, even after centuries of domestication, longs to live in a pack. If you take this as the bedrock fact of your pet's existence, then a lot of odd-seeming behavior suddenly becomes very understandable. In the wild, for instance, losing track of your companions could mean death. That's why dogs hate to see you leave, go berserk when you return, and may, out of fear, destroy things in your absence. This is also why, once you establish yourself as your dog's leader, it will strive to please you by accepting house-training and obedience training (see page 25).

and Why They Are, in Many Cases, Unbelievable

What, exactly, is a purebred dog? Mostly it's a figment of the imagination. Every dog breed is a mix of many different individuals, all blended together to create a particular look or mental attitude that can be transmitted reliably from one generation to the next. However, this kind of dog is in no way more "pure" (whatever that means) than any other canine on the planet.

The idea of breeding different kinds of dogs for different tasks goes back thousands of years. Examine old Assyrian ruins and you'll find engravings of very greyhound-like hunting dogs. And in Roman times armies were augmented with hulking war dogs that looked very much like mastiffs. But were they direct ancestors of *our* greyhounds and mastiffs? Maybe, maybe not.

Things got very muddled in the nineteenth century, when European and American dog breeders began creating canines not just to do useful work, but to conform to particular aesthetic standards. Before that time, the only standard that mattered was whether the dog in question could do its job. If a sheepdog could manage a herd, and a mastiff could fight bravely in battle, no one cared if they looked exactly like every other sheepdog or mastiff on the planet.

In the dog show world, the opposite became true. Often, whether a dog was good at hunting or herding mattered not a whit when it was led into the ring, felt up, marched around, and given a score. What mattered was how closely it conformed to its breed standard—a detailed, multipage template outlining what aficionados felt a representative of a particular type should look like, from the length of its tail to the color of its coat.

Any number of formerly purely working breeds were "prettied up" for the dog show circuit. For instance, to increase its eye-candy potential, the Irish setter was crossed with other types, including the elegant borzoi, to make it look more "refined." It didn't make it a better hunting dog (its original purpose), but it did help turn it into the glamorous redhead we know today. Even the Chihuahua was given some additional sturdiness by crossing it with everything from the papillon to various small terriers.

Which is why it's hard to say how closely today's purebreds are related to dogs from thousands, or even hundreds, of years ago. Examine the histories of many supposedly ancient breeds, and you'll often find that a lot of tinkering was done in the last 200 years to tweak them into the shapes we see now. So perhaps today's mastiffs are related to ancient war dogs. But if they are, given all the influences they've undergone since then, the relationship is probably about as close as that of Alexander the Great to a guy who runs a gyro stand in Cincinnati.

Not that this stops all sorts of fantastic claims from being made. It reminds one of the nouveaux riches who come into money and try to buy themselves hereditary titles to spice up their dreary family histories. For instance, for a long time the golden retriever was said to descend from a troupe of Russian circus dogs that toured England. And boosters of the Pharaoh hound (the locals on its native Malta know it by the less-exalted name of "rabbit dog") sometimes assert that its lineage dates back to ancient Egypt because it resembles canines shown in hieroglyphs. This is the equivalent of saying you must be related to British royalty because you have big ears and funny-looking teeth.

Which is not to say that a handful of breeds don't go back hundreds, even thousands, of years. In a few cases, such as with the basenji, or African bark-less dog, this can be proved. The basenji was brought to the West from Central Africa in the mid-twentieth century in a series of carefully documented expeditions. And it does appear that the tiny Pekingese was for centuries a favorite of Chinese royalty.

The process of "refining" purebreds continues, for better or worse. These days, because so few dogs actually work for a living, almost everything is for show. The collie, for instance, keeps sprouting an ever longer, ever more narrow, ever more "aesthetically pleasing" nose. The only problem is that this forces its eyes to get smaller and smaller, giving these dogs compromised vision. As usual, none of this makes the collie a better herder, guardian, or friend. It just gives it a bigger honker.

What purebreds *aren't* is a pack of genetically enhanced überdogs that are superior to other canines. What they *are* is a group of animals created through controlled breeding to reliably reproduce a set of physical and mental traits useful for work, companionship, or the show ring. The American Kennel Club (AKC) divides them into seven major classifications: sporting dogs, working dogs, toys, terriers, hounds, herding dogs, and nonsporting dogs. Here's what you'll find in each.

Sporting Dogs. This niche is home to most of the world's spaniels, pointers, setters, and retrievers. In short, any dog that was once (and, more often than not, still is) used to locate game, flush game, and/or retrieve game. For the most part, these breeds (including the Weimaraner, golden retriever, and Labrador retriever) are famous for their energy and buoyant personalities—as well as their need for tremendous amounts of exercise.

Working Dogs. This category holds most of the famous guard and service breeds, including the Great Dane, Doberman pinscher, Rottweiler, and Alaskan malamute. If it can bite your arm off or pull a sled all the way to the North Pole, it's probably here. Just remember that these dogs are big, powerful, and need lots of training and socialization to make them good citizens. If you don't have the time or the intestinal fortitude to cope with such a demanding animal, pick something else.

Toys. Most of the yippy little lapdogs reside in this category, including the Chihuahua, Shih Tzu, and Pomeranian. While most other canines were bred to handle a particular job, many of these were developed merely to serve as tiny, cuddly companions. However, these dogs are more than living, breathing accent pillows. Some, such as the Chihuahua and the Pomeranian, have peppery personalities and very well-developed Napoleon complexes. Some may even, believe it or not, try to dominate a weak owner.

Terriers. The smaller members of this bloody-minded clan, such as the cairn and Jack Russell, were bred to pursue animals into their lairs and then kick their butts in close combat (hence the name terrier, which means "earth dog"). Larger versions, including the bull terrier and American Staffordshire terrier, were created to kick the crap out of *anything*, whether it's in its lair or not. Terriers possess some of the dog world's most vivacious personalities. Unfortunately, they can also cause unending grief in the hands of a weak, disinterested, or overly aggressive owner. They like to dig. And fight other dogs. And chase small animals (including cats). And bark. So you'll have lots to cover in obedience class.

Hounds. These dogs trail game either by scent (bloodhounds, beagles, basset hounds), by sight (Afghans, greyhounds, borzois), or both (basenjis). Sight and scent hounds tend to diverge in interesting ways. Scent hunters are generally big, snuffling galoots with immense noses and floppy ears (it's sometimes said the ears help "concentrate" scents and guide them toward the nostrils). Sight hounds are streamlined, elegant-looking, and capable of pursuing prey at high speed over open country. On one point they are the same, however. Both are easily distracted, and they may dart off after an interesting smell/sight without regard to their personal safety or to how many times you shout "No! No! Stay! Stay! Heel!" as they recede into the distance.

Herding Dogs. Developed to manage cattle, sheep, or both, these breeds are noted for their energy and extreme intelligence (apparently it takes lots of smarts to keep those clever ungulates in line). The category includes everything from the collie to the German shepherd, which was originally developed not for kicking butt, but for managing sheep. Herding dogs illustrate an important point: It is sometimes possible for a housebound dog to be too smart. Breeds such as the Border collie need lots of exercise and mental stimulation, or they may make their own fun by causing property damage or by developing bizarre, obsessive-compulsive behaviors. If you don't have the time or energy to serve as a herder's personal entertainment center, pick something else.

Nonsporting Dogs. This mixed bag encompasses some very odd littermates, from the bichon frise to the bulldog to the Dalmatian. What do they have in common? Nothing, save their membership in the nonsporting category.

Here are some key points to consider when trying to find the right breed for you and yours. Remember to take your time, because you'll probably live with your choice for a decade or more.

Size. Some larger dogs, such as the golden retriever, can do quite well in apartments, so long as they receive proper exercise. However, in general, the bigger the canine, the bigger the accommodations it requires. For instance, even the most undemanding Great Pyrenees (which can weigh as much as 125 pounds) takes up a lot of space. It's like owning a big piece of furniture—a piece of furniture that drools.

Coat Type. One of the most overlooked issues of dog ownership is that of shedding. Many breeds, particularly those with thick "double coats" (including the Siberian husky and schipperke) will undergo massive seasonal shedding in spring and fall, sloughing off enough hair to (no exaggeration) fill several grocery bags. Some dogs, such as the Weimaraner and Rhodesian ridgeback, shed year round—and their short hair can be very tough to get out of upholstery and clothing. Other breeds, such as the collie and Afghan hound, have coats that require regular home care, plus professional grooming. Still others, such as the poodle, don't shed at all (though they still require grooming).

Temperament. To find an ideal canine companion, it's vital that you spend at least as much time evaluating candidates' mental traits as you do their looks. Because looks can be deceiving. For instance, the dachshund looks like a lapdog but is in fact an attitude-filled former hunter whose name means "badger dog" in German. And the dangerous-looking Siberian husky is in most cases mellow, overly friendly with strangers, and next-to-useless as a watchdog.

Exercise Requirements. While some canines (the Chihuahua, the bichon frise) need very little exercise simply because they are very little, other breeds can demand a significant commitment of time and sweat. The greyhound must have regular walks and regular runs. The basset hound needs its workouts to keep from putting on weight. And a Border collie needs not only exercise, but mental stimulation. A dog that's denied its outdoor time will soon become unhealthy—and may turn buggy from boredom. Remember, simply turning your dog out into the yard doesn't count as exercise. Left to itself, the typical canine would do just what you would do—find a shady spot and go to sleep.

Potential Genetic Issues. Investigating the sorts of problems your favorite breed is heir to is important for a couple of reasons. It can save you the grief of falling in love with a puppy, only to see its life cut short by some terrible disease. Also, it can help you understand (and, in some cases, prevent) those problems. For instance, if you get a big, deep-chested breed like the Great Dane, you'll have to learn all about the horrible condition known as bloat (see page 22). Remember, just because a breed is prone to a certain ailment doesn't mean your dog will get it. It's just something you need to be aware of. You can lessen your chances greatly by working with a careful breeder.

Schedule Demands. Some dogs, such as the golden retriever, don't mind if you leave them alone all day. But some (such as the vizsla) really, really do— and they'll misbehave until you get the point. Also, if you don't have time to train a puppy, you might want to consider getting an already-trained adult dog. Remember, however, that even canines that can be by themselves for a while don't want to be alone all the time. Your dog, no matter the breed, will always claim a healthy amount of your attention.

Financial Demands. Caring for even the smallest canine will cost hundreds of dollars annually for food and veterinary visits. For obvious reasons, the price increases right along with the size of the dog. Also, unexpected medical problems can drive costs into four figures. Are you prepared for such a potential financial drain?

Familial Obligations. First, make sure everyone in your family wants to get a dog. Next, make sure the canine you select is appropriate for your family. Remember that a very large dog might bowl over small children or older adults and that a smaller breed is probably inappropriate for houses with very young children. It might be injured or might nip at the kids. Finally, never get a pet as a surprise gift for anyone. Such "surprises" often wind up at the pound.

Obtaining a quality representative of many of the breeds listed in this book can be a long, involved, and, quite often, expensive process. Which is exactly as it should be. If it isn't a pain, then something is probably wrong.

Here's why. Because purebreds are subject to numerous genetic disorders (see page 22), careful breeders take great pains to match only healthy males to healthy females, which hopefully produces healthy puppies. That's why pretty much the only person you should acquire a puppy from is a careful breeder. The best place to find them is through references from breed clubs and veterinarians. Good ones aren't in this to earn money, because if they do it right, they generally don't make a dime. Breeders can provide a complete medical history of your puppy's parents and relevant medical data about the puppy itself, and they can put you in touch with others who have acquired their dogs. Most tellingly, a good breeder will have questions for *you*, including why you want this particular breed, your expertise with canines, and your family status and living arrangements. In many cases, breeders will stipulate that if at any time you must give up the dog, you have to return it to them.

After all this is accomplished, you may wait six months or longer for a puppy, for which you could pay hundreds of dollars.

Of course there are other places to get dogs. Lots of people buy "purebreds" from pet stores. But don't *you* do it. These animals are usually the products of puppy mills—despicable places where canines with questionable genetic backgrounds are kept under brutal conditions and turned into puppy-making factories. The dogs thus produced are almost invariably poorly socialized and loaded with mental and physical defects. Trouble like that you do not need.

Buying a dog from a "backyard breeder" (the kind who takes out tiny newspaper ads saying, for instance, "Boxer pups 10wks $100") is equally dicey and disreputable. The puppies can be just as genetically questionable as their pet-store siblings, and the people who sell them are generally ignorant yahoos out to make a quick buck. They won't ask you about your qualifications for owning one of their dogs. They will ask if you want to pay by cash or check.

Last but certainly not least, there's one other excellent source for pure-breds—breed rescue services. These are groups of dog enthusiasts who make it their business to find new homes for abandoned dogs of particular breeds—everything from Pekingese to German shepherds to whippets. You name the dog, and there's almost certainly a service looking out for it (see Appendix). These volunteers (they're almost all volunteers) get dogs out of shelters and abusive situations, place them in foster homes, then canvass the nation for new, more responsible owners.

Which is where you come in. If you contact one of these services, expect to go through a lengthy pre-adoption screening process. These dogs were already booted out of one home, and the rescue folks don't want to repeat that trauma. Then, if you're deemed worthy, you may have to drive or fly quite a distance to pick up your pet. But you'll have the dog of your dreams, and the dog will have the home of *its* dreams. So everybody's happy.

One of the biggest problems with purebred dogs is that the same selective breeding that magnifies desirable traits may also increase the chances for genetic illnesses. Almost every purebred is prone to at least one such hereditary disorder, and many are prone to an entire laundry list. Here are some of the most common.

Allergies. Allergic reactions are caused when the dog's immune system over-reacts to a specific environmental factor—an allergen. Some purebreds (among them the bichon frise, pug, and boxer) are prone to allergy-induced skin conditions and gastrointestinal disorders. Grass, flea bites, even certain dog food ingredients can act as triggers.

Back Problems. Many breeds can suffer from such disorders, which include, but are not confined to, slipped disks. Dachshunds, corgis, and Dandie Dinmont terriers are among the leading sufferers. In general, the longer the dog's back, the greater the dog's potential for back problems.

Bloat. This is an extremely dangerous condition common among big, deep-chested dogs such as Saint Bernards and Great Danes. Canines that eat too fast or too much, or that exercise vigorously after a meal, may experience a sudden buildup of gas that causes the stomach to rotate, sealing it at both ends like a sausage link. Symptoms include repeated unproductive retching, panting, and obvious pain. Only emergency surgery can correct this condition, and only the feeding of several small meals a day, and the avoidance of strenuous activity before and after those meals, can prevent it. If you get a large breed, talk to your veterinarian about the best ways to prevent bloat.

Deafness. This issue bedevils several breeds, including Dalmatians, Great Pyrenees, and bull terriers. If a dog can't hear, it is virtually impossible to train—which is why many deaf puppies are destroyed shortly after birth.

Diabetes. This condition is caused by the body's inability to produce or use insulin, the hormone that converts sugars and starches into energy. It's a fairly common problem in dachshunds, among other breeds.

Eye Disorders. Purebreds can face a very wide range of eye issues, from cataracts (extremely common) to night blindness. For instance, the Chinese shar-pei is vulnerable to inverted eyelids, and the poodle and Rottweiler are prone to blindness caused by cataracts or progressive retinal atrophy.

Heart Disorders. Difficulties range from premature deterioration of the heart muscle to misshapen heart valves. Such problems are often seen in boxers, bulldogs, and King Charles spaniels.

Hip Dysplasia. This defect causes abnormal positioning of the hip joint bones, often leading to great discomfort and arthritis. In general, the larger the breed, the more common the problem. Dogs can also suffer from a related condition called elbow dysplasia.

Rage Syndrome. A largely untreatable genetic defect sometimes seen in poorly bred cocker spaniels and springer spaniels. Dogs afflicted with it suffer epileptic-like fits, except that instead of seizing, they go into spasms of uncontrolled aggression. The only way to avoid this problem is to acquire a carefully bred dog.

Skin Disorders. Different breeds can display many different skin disorders, including strong reactions to particular allergens (see Allergies, above). Boxers are subject to an entire raft of skin tumors and cysts, the Chinese shar-pei's wrinkled skin leaves it vulnerable to numerous infections, and the Dalmatian can develop a poorly understood, coat-discoloring problem known by the extremely unappetizing name of "Dal crud."

In Praise of Mutts

If the thought of cooling your heels on a waiting list and then shelling out hundreds of dollars doesn't appeal to you, then don't do it. Because there's one type of dog that's always available in great numbers, near your home, for a nominal fee—the mixed breed, a.k.a. the Heinz 57, the mongrel, or the mutt.

About 75 percent of the dogs languishing in animal shelters are mutts—the products of indiscriminate, unsupervised mating between various types of canines. What does one get from such haphazard pairings? A dog that is often, in important ways, superior to the world's finest purebreds.

The biggest advantage is health. Mutts are usually more physically sound than purebreds, many of whom have for generations been bred (and sometimes inbred) in a very restricted way. Splashing around in an ankle-deep gene pool can be dangerous. While controlled breeding can accentuate a desired trait, such as long, silky hair, it can also inadvertently magnify genetic disorders, such as hip dysplasia or a propensity to develop bizarre cancers. Almost every purebred has a couple of genetic foibles. Some have a lot.

Not so with mutts. Their generalized constitution makes them tough targets for such purebred bugaboos. There's just one drawback. While one can make some fairly strong generalizations about the personalities of different purebreds (if you couldn't, this book wouldn't exist), mutts must always be taken on a case-by-case basis. For instance, a chow chow/golden retriever mix might look terrifying, but have a playful, harmless demeanor. Or it may look harmless and have a terrifying demeanor. Or it could have something in between. You just don't know— which is why it's important to spend plenty of pre-adoption time with a mutt, gauging its personality.

But if you find a good one (and there are thousands of good ones out there) it will lavish you with all the love and attention any purebred could ever give. And you never know what treasures you might stumble across. After all, the Boykin spaniel, now a popular American hunting and companion dog, traces its roots to an adopted stray named Dumpy.

What's it like to be a dog? Imagine watching a movie in a foreign language, with no subtitles. You may get the gist of the plot, but you'll never fully understand what's going on. That's what the average canine faces every day of its life. This animal, originally meant to live in the wilderness among its own kind, instead must consort with a family of bipeds and regularly confront such unfathomable concepts as vet visits, vacuum cleaners, mail carriers, and hair bows. In order to survive, this four-legged stranger in a strange land must rely on its owner for guidance in even the simplest matters. Which means that, for its comfort and safety, it must be carefully trained. These are the "big four" areas that need to be covered.

Socialization. This is the very first thing that must be drummed into a puppy's head. From a very early age, it should be introduced (in a positive, utterly nonthreatening way) to strange people, strange situations, and strange animals. For instance, if you want your dog to get along with cats, this is the time to arrange a mixer. For breeds that tend to be combative or naturally suspicious (chow chows, Rottweilers, Dobermans), this sort of early experience is vital. Be warned that negative puppyhood experiences can shape a grown-up dog's character just as strongly as positive ones. A puppy who has an unhappy encounter with a man wearing a hat may fear men in hats (or men in general) forevermore.

House-training. Each dog listing in this book includes a section called "Bladder Matters," in which any special house-training problems peculiar to that breed are outlined. If there aren't any, we often use the phrase "No special house-training problems." We never say "Easy to house-train," because that would be a lie. Teaching a puppy to potty outdoors is almost always a laborious process requiring patience, vigilance, and lots of time. Entire books have been written on this subject. If you've never house-trained a dog before, we recommend talking to your veterinarian, and perhaps buying one of those books on the subject. House-training is a big deal and demands a lot of attention. This is one of the main reasons why adopting an adult, already-trained dog can be so attractive.

Dominance. Dogs are pack animals, and packs are hierarchies. The strongest, or "alpha" dog lords it over everyone. The second-strongest lords it over everyone but the alpha. The third strongest . . . well, you get the idea. It is very important that, early on, you establish yourself (along with every other two-legged member of your household) as your dog's superior. Do this properly and your canine will happily play Ed McMahon to your Johnny Carson. But if you neglect to establish dominance, you could create real problems. If your dog is a Jack Russell terrier, you could face a nippy, snarling little animal who thinks it runs the show. If your dog is a Doberman, you could face a nippy, snarling big dog who *knows* it runs the show.

Fortunately, there are many ways to establish authority over even the most powerful breed. Taking a dog to obedience classes and putting it through its paces is a strongly dominant move. Simply setting out its food every day is another strong gesture. But being firm and consistent is the most effective power play of all. Corporal punishment (striking or spanking) is definitely a bad idea. First, it can make a dog overly fearful or overly aggressive. Second, it ignores the fact that establishing dominance over a canine is basically a mind game. If it were all about physical force, puny humans wouldn't stand a chance against Rottweilers and mastiffs. Even a small breed like a Scottish terrier or basenji could inflict a breathtaking amount of damage on a human being if it feels like it. So make sure it never feels like it.

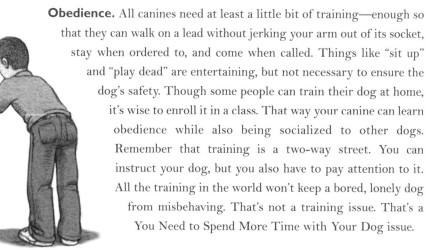

Obedience. All canines need at least a little bit of training—enough so that they can walk on a lead without jerking your arm out of its socket, stay when ordered to, and come when called. Things like "sit up" and "play dead" are entertaining, but not necessary to ensure the dog's safety. Though some people can train their dog at home, it's wise to enroll it in a class. That way your canine can learn obedience while also being socialized to other dogs. Remember that training is a two-way street. You can instruct your dog, but you also have to pay attention to it. All the training in the world won't keep a bored, lonely dog from misbehaving. That's not a training issue. That's a You Need to Spend More Time with Your Dog issue.

MEET THE BREEDS

Information for this book was gleaned primarily from representatives of various breed groups and, first and foremost, from breed rescue organization volunteers. These folks provided particularly useful insights, since they are painfully familiar with the sorts of behavioral issues and physical foibles that can land dogs in shelters.

As you peruse the entries, please remember that the descriptions of personalities and character traits are generalizations. Don't bite our heads off if the behaviors ascribed to certain breeds don't perfectly jibe with the representatives of that breed that you've encountered. We understand that, somewhere out there in the big world, there is indeed a basset hound that doesn't drool, a golden retriever that makes an excellent watchdog, and a quiet, laid-back sheltie. But they aren't the norm.

Each entry begins with a box listing the breed's vital statistics—weight, height, build, and coat type, followed by as much useful information as can be compressed onto one or two pages. All this dog data is broken down into the following categories:

Vital Stats	Weight, height, build, and other physical specifications.
The Incredible Origin	How the breed came to be.
Trademark Traits	A thumbnail sketch of the typical dog's emotional makeup.
Headaches and Hassles	Potential pains such as shedding, drooling, etc.
Special Perks	Outstanding features.
Bugs in the System	Genetic diseases and other physical shortcomings.
If someone broke into my house, this dog would	Watchdog and bodyguard skills.
If you like the (insert breed name here), check out	One or two possible canine alternatives.
Who should get this dog?	The ideal owner for a particular dog variety.

Consider Yourself Warned

This book lists slightly more than 100 varieties, including many of the most popular breeds, some up-and-comers, and a handful of interesting oddities. But while each dog is unique, the following caveats apply to pretty much all of them.

1 **If you do not obtain your dog from a responsible source, such as a careful breeder, rescue service, or animal shelter, the information in this book will not be as useful.** When we say that a particular dog breed is usually good with kids or has a placid demeanor or is easily trained, we mean a well-bred, well-socialized dog is all those things. Reputable breeders only work with high-quality animals, and shelters and rescue services make sure the dogs they offer to the public are adequately socialized and, to some degree, trained. If you get your pet from a backyard breeder or pet store, all bets are off.

2 **When we say a dog is "good with children," we mean respectful, well-mannered children over the age of, say, 8.** Even the most patient dog shouldn't be subjected to ear-pulling, tail-grabbing toddlers and may react badly to undisciplined kids of any age who tease or torment it. In general, young children should never be left alone with dogs, no matter how placid the canine may seem. This is simply too much to ask of any breed.

3 **Last but by no means least, you will notice that the words "well-trained and well-socialized" are used about 10 million times in these pages.** That's because all the rules of positive behavior apply only to dogs that are responsibly managed. Many breeds have long lists of potentially annoying behavior quirks, but if a dog is well-trained and well-socialized, many of these issues will simply go away or never manifest at all. Dogs generally become problems only in the hands of a weak, lazy, or disinterested owner. If you buy a dog and then ignore it, you're asking, at best, for an unruly canine. If you do this to a big, strong, naturally aggressive guarding breed . . . well, you might want to put 911 on your speed dial. Just in case.

How to Use the Icons: Dog Traits

To provide a snapshot of the particular issues and behaviors associated with specific dog varieties, the following icons can be found throughout the various breed descriptions.

DOG ICON	DESCRIPTION
S M L XL	**Size Matters:** Use these icons to determine if a breed is small (5–20 pounds or 2.26–9 kg), medium (21–60 pounds or 9.5–27.2 kg), large (61–100 pounds or 27.6–45.3 kg), or extra large (more than 100 pounds or 45.3 kg).
	Aggressive: May attempt to dominate a weak owner, display a marked distrust of strangers, and/or possess a higher-than-average drive to defend its territory. Remember, however, that just because a dog may show some aggressive tendencies doesn't mean it makes a bad pet.
	Good Watchdog: If someone breaks into your house, this dog will likely take some sort of definitive action, either raising the alarm by barking, confronting the intruder, or both.
	Very Smart: A more accurate term would be "very trainable," because many canine experts think there's little difference in brain power among the breeds. However, some are more eager to please their masters or predisposed to perform behaviors humans find useful or entertaining. Therefore, we think they're "smarter." Of course, brains are not always a good thing. A smart dog is a busy dog.
	Needs Lots of Grooming: Either the dog requires a complicated hairstyle, needs daily brushing, sheds truly horrifying amounts of hair, or all three.
	House-training Issues: This procedure can be a pain with almost any dog, but some breeds can have a particularly hard time.
	Numerous or Pronounced Genetic Defects: Almost all purebreds have at least a few genetic issues developed through generations of selective breeding. Some have such drastic problems that they should be taken into account by anyone interested in that particular variety.
	Can Make a Lot of Noise: Some breeds never quite realize that they don't have to bark at every person who passes on the sidewalk in front of their homes. Others, unless properly trained, may become "recreational barkers" who make noise simply to amuse themselves.
	Likes to Dig: Many breeds, particularly terriers, possess an instinctive urge to excavate. You'll need to monitor their backyard jaunts, unless you want your landscaping turned upside down.

Not every dog is right for every person or living arrangement. For instance, even the most mellow, pliant mastiff would be out of place in an efficiency apartment. And the Italian greyhound, because it's as fragile as an origami crane, makes a less-than-ideal playmate for kids, no matter how careful they try to be. To help you decide which canine is good for your particular situation, the following icons will be included, where appropriate, with the entries for various breeds.

A couple of caveats. In some cases a breed may be pegged as ideal for both couch potatoes and active people. This is because some dogs are such crowd pleasers that they will follow whatever lead their owner sets. Also, the icon for an "active" person doesn't just signify someone with the physical stamina to take the dog on long workouts. It can also signify that potential owners should have enough moxie to handle the workout a big and/or active breed can give *them*.

OWNER ICON	DESCRIPTION
	Suburbanite: An individual or family residing in a quiet neighborhood and possessing a fenced yard.
	City Dweller: An urban apartment dweller with access to a park or greenway.
	Family: The classic nuclear unit, complete with kids over the age of 8.
	Single Person: A bachelor, bachelorette, divorcée, widow, etc.
	Active: A high-energy individual who, perhaps, likes to run or participate in sports.
	Couch Potato: The sort of person who has his or her own distinctive buttprint worn into the sofa.
	Elderly: Retirees and empty nesters who live on their own.

Weight: *6–9 pounds (2.7–4.1 kg).* **Height:** *9–11 inches (22.9–27.9 cm).* **Build:** *Sturdy frame with large, flat-faced head.* **Coat:** *Stiff, shaggy black hair.* **Brains:** *Smart and relatively easy to train.* **Bladder Matters:** *Can be somewhat difficult to house-train.*

The Incredible Origin: This little dog's odd, vaguely simian face (the translation of its name is something like "monkey-faced biter") makes it look about as practical and functional as a unicorn. But it's no mere toy. Originally bred in Germany, it was created to exterminate rats and even to track game in open country—which must have been an extremely amusing sight. Perhaps its quarry, rather than dropping from exhaustion, simply died of embarrassment after being chased through the woods by an "opponent" looking only slightly less whimsical than a Pokémon character. Almost wiped out in World War II (because the breeding process is difficult, and many Europeans were too busy saving their own lives to worry about this dog's future), the "affen," also known as The Black Devil, has made a mild comeback as a companion dog.

Trademark Traits: The affen makes a good apartment pet as long as you can control its penchant for barking. It's lively and curious, but its exercise needs can be satisfied with occasional walks and a romp around the living room. Also, if you have a rodent problem, you won't have it for long.

Headaches and Hassles: The affen sheds, and has a great affinity for barking. Particularly high-strung individuals may announce the arrival of guests by launching into an unnerving, high-pitched yipping fit. Even after the noise subsides, they can remain suspicious and testy around new faces. They can get snappy with other dogs, and can lash out at human strangers who invade their personal space.

Special Perks: Whether it's prancing down the street with its high-stepping gait or wrestling with toys on the living room floor, the affen provides a lot of entertainment in a very small package. Its coat, though somewhat prone to matting, is fairly easy to maintain. Also, it's more sturdy and robust than many toy

DOG TRAITS

WHO SHOULD GET THIS DOG?

Someone with a lot of money and patience. Affens are relatively rare, so acquiring a carefully bred puppy can take time—not to mention a handful of Benjamins. They aren't good with very small children, who may get nipped if they treat them roughly. Also, affen puppies are much too fragile to be handled by a child.

OWNER TRAITS

dogs, though when it comes to animals this size, "robust" is a relative term. It's like saying that one type of stemware is less prone to breakage than another. Never forget that though the affen may think it is invincible, it is still a tiny animal that could be seriously injured if it were stepped on, sat on, or dropped. It won't hesitate to tangle with strange dogs, so it must always be leashed in public.

Bugs in the System: Generally healthy, but susceptible to eye problems.

If someone broke into my house, this dog would: Stand its ground, barking furiously. Affens are considered excellent watchdogs, because they're possessive of their homes and know no fear. They like to stay on top of things by investigating new sounds, no matter how innocuous, and by carefully reconnoitering any physical change in their surroundings. It's kind of like living with the world's most paranoid shopping mall security guard.

If you like the affenpinscher, check out: The Brussels griffon, which possesses the same monkeylike face, or the Pomeranian, which has the same take-no-prisoners attitude.

Afghan Hound

Weight: *45–65 pounds (20.3–29.3 kg).* **Height:** *24–29 inches (61.0–73.7 cm).* **Build:** *Sleek and muscular.* **Coat:** *Thick, long, silky hair in numerous colors and color combinations.* **Brains:** *Very intelligent, but it takes a great deal of time and persistence to get it to apply its brains to training.* **Bladder Matters:** *No particular house-training issues.*

The Incredible Origin: Evidence suggests that dogs like this have been running around the inhospitable wastes of Afghanistan for thousands of years, doing everything from hunting gazelle and snow leopards to guarding flocks. Today's Afghan is primarily a show dog and pet, though it's probably *too* popular of a pet. Beginning in the 1970s it won fame as a fashion accessory—a disaster for this breed, which needs a great deal more attention and maintenance than, say, a Prada purse.

Trademark Traits: The Afghan is very independent and reserved—almost haughty—around strangers. With its family, however, it will let its long, long hair down, acting jolly and cutting up. From them (and only them) it demands a great deal of love and attention. Though it is incredibly athletic outdoors, indoors it can be content to lounge for hours in a comfortable chair—a chair that will soon be coated with hair.

Headaches and Hassles: There's no way to soft-pedal this. The Afghan's long, luxurious coat requires a great deal of maintenance—maintenance that *must* be done, lest the dog turn into a matted mess. A routine bath can involve an armload of towels, a blow-dryer, combs, conditioner, and a lot of time. Of course you can leave this to a professional, but it will cost you a fortune, and it won't get you out of regular home comb-outs. Dedicated owners even put long hoods (called "snoods") around their dogs' heads and necks at dinnertime, to keep their coats out of their bowls.

Afghans must be kept leashed in public, and their yard must be surrounded by a *high* fence. We're talking medium-security prison high. These dogs run like the wind and can leap to extraordinary heights. If they see something interesting they will vanish. They are problematic around cats and other small animals.

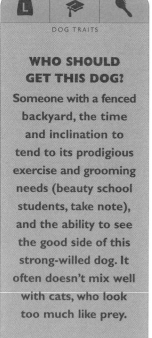

DOG TRAITS

WHO SHOULD GET THIS DOG?

Someone with a fenced backyard, the time and inclination to tend to its prodigious exercise and grooming needs (beauty school students, take note), and the ability to see the good side of this strong-willed dog. It often doesn't mix well with cats, who look too much like prey.

OWNER TRAITS

Special Perks: The well-cared-for Afghan truly is a showstoppingly beautiful companion animal. Plus, their long hair is fairly easy to spot and remove from upholstery—unlike the shorter hair of some dogs, which can become snared in the weave.

Bugs in the System: Though properly bred Afghans are usually healthy, they can suffer from hip dysplasia and various eye problems, including cataracts. Also, in hot weather these dogs are, for obvious reasons, prone to heat exhaustion. They aren't distance runners, so they don't make good jogging partners.

If someone broke into my house, this dog would: Do little if anything. These dogs may be mortal enemies of snow leopards, but they're clueless about housebreakers.

If you like the Afghan, check out: The borzoi and saluki, both of which are just as fast as the Afghan and require almost as much grooming. Or, if choking on pet hair isn't your thing, consider the swift but short-coated greyhound.

Weight: 50–70 pounds (22.5–31.5 kg). *Height:* 22–24 inches (55.9–61.0 cm). *Build:* Lithe but powerful body. *Coat:* Dense, wiry, tan-colored coat with black around the torso and neck. *Brains:* Extremely intelligent. *Bladder Matters:* No special house-training problems.

The Incredible Origin: Developed in the valley of the Aire in Yorkshire, England, to help the locals hunt otter, this biggest of all terrier breeds has, over the decades, been employed as everything from a police dog to a hunting dog to a four-legged, frontline messenger during World War I. These days the Airedale's natural habitat is the living room rug.

Trademark Traits: With its fancy haircut and aristocratic good looks, this breed seems like a fantastic drawing room accessory. Nothing could be further from the truth. Airedales, like most terriers, were bred to hunt and fight, and even the most refined specimens still harbor a strong desire (which they will indulge at any opportunity) to dig, wrestle, run, brawl, and chase. As physically strong as it is strong-willed, a fired-up Airedale can be as frenetic as a 3-year-old in the throes of a sugar rush.

Headaches and Hassles: Just about everything to do with the Airedale is high maintenance. It is energetic and inquisitive, and it requires lots of exercise and face time with its owners (the word "needy" comes to mind). Careful socialization and training is mandatory for puppies, who are famous for, among other things, never staying still unless they are asleep, destructive chewing, barking, and digging. Training an Airedale can be a long and sometimes frustrating process, but you'll need to get a handle on these problems (particularly the chewing and digging) before the dog reaches adult size. Airedales are also dedicated crotch sniffers, so you might want to warn guests. This breed likes to chase things and can pick fights with other dogs, so it can never be trusted off its lead in public. Also, if you want your Airedale to look like an Airedale, you'll have to have it groomed professionally. Its famous beard becomes soaked with water whenever it takes a

DOG TRAITS

WHO SHOULD GET THIS DOG?

A family or individual willing to give it the attention and careful training it requires to become a good citizen. Remember that the typical Airedale will never be content to pile up on the couch every evening and vegetate. If that's your idea of a fun night in, consider another breed.

OWNER TRAITS

drink—a problem the typical Airedale solves by rubbing its sodden snout on a rug or the nearest piece of furniture. Finally, neat freaks take note: This dog loves puddles and mud.

Special Perks: Airedales (the well-trained, well-socialized ones, at least) tend to calm down after their second birthdays. They can accept even the most complicated training, and they display great loyalty to their families. They are also highly entertaining companions, forever performing attention-grabbing stunts.

Bugs in the System: In general, this breed has few genetic problems. Hip dysplasia is occasionally seen, as is gastroenteritis and eczema.

If someone broke into my house, this dog would: In many cases, attack ferociously and without mercy. Like most terrier breeds, it makes an excellent home guardian. Most troublemakers would be warned off by its bark alone.

If you like Airedales, check out: The fox terrier, which offers all the personality traits of this breed but in a slightly smaller (though no less energetic and rowdy) package.

Akita

Weight: 90–110 pounds (40.5–49.5 kg). **Height:** 24–28 inches (61.0–71.1 cm). **Build:** Very stocky and powerful. Imagine a German shepherd on steroids. Very distinctive curled, bristly tail. **Coat:** Thick, heavy coat in a wide range of color mixes. **Brains:** Highly intelligent—though they may not wish to apply their smarts to the tasks you give them. **Bladder Matters:** No special house-training issues.

The Incredible Origin: This ancient Japanese breed (it hails from the Akita region of the island of Honshu) has been used for everything from hunting to guarding to fighting to police work. It was introduced to the United States after World War II and popularized by the renowned Helen Keller (her dog was nicknamed Kami, and he traveled with Keller on the lecturing circuit). Since then its popularity has grown steadily. Today the breed, which was also formerly used to hunt bears, is primarily a home companion. It is also considered the national dog of Japan (in fact, when a person in Japan falls ill, friends will often send a small statue of an Akita to express their desires for a quick recovery).

Trademark Traits: The Akita served for generations as a pit fighter, so careful breeding was required to create a specimen gentle enough to use as a household pet. Modern, well-bred, and adequately socialized Akitas make good companions. However, inside each one beats the heart of a warrior. They are, of course, impeccable watchdogs and family guardians. Just don't expect them to cuddle up on the couch with you, learn a slew of endearing tricks, or fawn at your feet, begging for attention. If that's your bag, try a golden retriever. Also, for some reason, Akitas have webbed feet, which makes them excellent swimmers. It's an odd attribute for a fighting dog, but there it is.

Headaches and Hassles: The Akita's thick coat requires regular brushing, and during spring and fall it sheds in vacuum-choking, rug-coating wads. An Akita can be very suspicious of strangers (even benign ones) and aggressive toward other canines. It can also dominate an overly passive owner. Regular, lengthy walks are a must.

DOG TRAITS

WHO SHOULD GET THIS DOG?

A determined individual who can show the Akita (in a nonviolent way, of course) who's boss. A weak, passive person will be walked on (perhaps literally) by this powerful dog. This breed can be a devoted companion to, and guardian of, older children, but is definitely not a good choice for families with toddlers.

OWNER TRAITS

Special Perks: A well-trained Akita is probably more effective than most home security systems available on the market. Some owners claim this breed also possesses a near-clairvoyant ability to tell "good people" from "bad people." So if your dog seems less than enthused about a new acquaintance, take note.

Bugs in the System: The breed is prone to hip dysplasia, thyroid problems, knee disorders, skin and eye conditions, and diseases of the immune system.

If someone broke into my house, this dog would: Treat the intruder to a heaping helping of pain, with a side order of regret. This sort of thing is literally what Akitas were made for.

If you like Akitas, check out: The German shepherd, which also excels at home defense.

*Weight: 70–95 pounds (31.5–42.8 kg). **Height:** 22–26 inches (55.9–66.0 cm). **Build:** Stocky and powerful. **Coat:** Thick, bristly double coat in a mix of shades (though the face is always white). **Brains:** This breed is smart and can learn a lot—if it feels like it. The problem is, even a well-trained malamute will disregard commands whenever the spirit moves it. **Bladder Matters:** Can be tricky to house-train.*

The Incredible Origin: Used as a sled dog by North American Inuit tribes, this hardy canine has gone all the way to the North Pole as part of exploration teams. Though the snowmobile put it out of a job, it's still a popular pet.

Trademark Traits: In spite of their ferocious, wolflike appearance, malamutes are usually friendly, happy dogs. They like to play, and are friendly and loving with their master, their master's family . . . and pretty much every other human on earth as well. They will, however, try to dominate a weak owner, and are prone to roughhousing.

Headaches and Hassles: This dog's thick, thick coat requires regular grooming. Its hair will come out by the handful during the peak spring and fall shedding seasons. Bored or poorly trained malamutes can take a house apart faster than a rock star can trash a hotel room. They are also experts at snatching interesting (translation: edible) items off counters, out of cabinets, even off seemingly inaccessible shelves. These dogs are bred for long-distance running, so they need lots of exercise. However, because they're not too good about following commands, they can never be trusted off their lead in public. Also, be careful about taking them rollerblading. If a malamute hits his stride, he may tow you into the next county. These dogs play hard and have a strong prey drive. They must be carefully socialized around children, and in most cases can't be trusted around cats and other small animals. Finally, malamutes like to dig. A lot. So if you like to garden, kiss that hobby good-bye.

Special Perks: The malamute's coat is peculiarly repellant to dirt and water. This breed usually doesn't bark excessively, though it

---

DOG TRAITS

WHO SHOULD GET THIS DOG?

An individual or family with a big yard, plenty of time to exercise the dog, and plenty of patience for its antics. Remember that the malamute is inappropriate for homes with very young children and can have big problems with small animals, such as cats.

OWNER TRAITS

does emit a wide range of highly entertaining noises, often "talking" at great length to its owner. It is also immune to even the bitterest cold—though this is not an excuse to leave it outside for extended periods. Like all family pets, this breed belongs in the family home. Ignoring it is a surefire recipe for behavior problems.

Bugs in the System: For obvious reasons, this breed fares about as well in warm climates as a snowball in hell. They can also suffer from eye problems and hip dysplasia, and are especially susceptible to bloat, because they will bolt massive quantities of food if allowed. Some malamutes can develop a strong-smelling coat—a condition called "coat funk."

If someone broke into my house, this dog would: Frighten any intruder with a brain in his head, largely because of its wolflike appearance. Unfortunately, this dog's appearance is the most threatening thing about it. Malamutes aren't particularly suspicious of strangers—even ones wearing ski masks.

If you like the Alaskan malamute, check out: The slightly smaller but equally fuzzy Siberian husky.

*Weight: 65–75 pounds (29.3–33.8 kg). **Height:** 21–25 inches (53.3–63.5 cm). **Build:** Trim and graceful. **Coat:** Dense, short hair in the typical "hound colors" of white, brown, black, etcetera. **Brains:** The foxhound is smart, but like many hounds it has a hard time paying attention during training sessions. Any interesting smell can distract it. **Bladder Matters:** House-training can take a while.*

The Incredible Origin: Developed during the eighteenth and nineteenth centuries (George Washington is said to have lent a hand), the American foxhound is basically a modification of the English foxhound that's been tweaked to make it more useful in North America.

Trademark Traits: As its spectacularly functional name demonstrates, the American foxhound is a working breed that has made few concessions to the modern world. Though placid and friendly, this isn't the sort of dog that will constantly bug you for attention. It will need careful training and socialization to adapt to home life.

Headaches and Hassles: The foxhound requires plenty of exercise—so much that it is inappropriate for apartment life. If denied an acceptable outlet for its energy, it may soon find an unacceptable one. Foxhounds, when excited, also emit an unbelievably unnerving bark/howl called a "bay." Make sure you experience this sound before getting this dog.

Special Perks: The coat is easy to maintain, and the dog's personality is laid-back and low-key. Sure it may ignore you sometimes, but it will likely never snap or bite. Also, this dog, which was bred to live in a pack, gets along well with other canines.

Bugs in the System: This is a very healthy breed, though hip and eye problems sometimes arise.

If someone broke into my house, this dog would: Bark, maybe. Or maybe not. Foxhounds just aren't cut out for guard duty.

If you like the American foxhound, check out: A hound that's much more amenable to home life—the trusty beagle.

DOG TRAITS

WHO SHOULD GET THIS DOG?

A family or individual with a fenced yard and the willingness to commit a lot of time to training and long, long walks. Actually, unless your name is Cletus and you like to hunt varmints, this all-business breed probably isn't for you.

OWNER TRAITS

Weight: *40–50 pounds (18.0–22.5 kg).* **Height:** *15–16 inches (38.1–40.6 cm).* **Build:** *Powerful, stocky body.* **Coat:** *Extremely short hair most commonly in brindle, black, and red.* **Brains:** *Good AmStaffs are very loyal and reasonably trainable (thank God). However, they're not all that bright.* **Bladder Matters:** *No special house-training issues.*

The Incredible Origin: Developed from the English Staffordshire bull terrier, which was created for pit fighting and bullbaiting, the Americanized model is (surprise, surprise) bigger, stronger, and even more indestructible than its old-world ancestor.

Trademark Traits: Well-bred "AmStaffs" can be placid, steady pets. Poorly bred AmStaffs (including their no-good, half-breed cousin, the pit bull) are disasters waiting to happen. The thing to remember is that these animals were made for battle, not tea parties. They can pull thousands of pounds, bite through chain-link fences, and, if provoked, fight savagely until either they or (far more likely) their opponent dies. They can never be trusted, unleashed and unmonitored, around strangers or other animals. *Never.*

Headaches and Hassles: There is absolutely no limit to the mischief a bored or irritated AmStaff can do. They can gnaw through walls, tear gaping holes in fences, and carry around cement lawn ornaments in their mouths as if they were rawhide bones. Toys will divert this energy, but not just any toy. Since their jaws can crush a human femur in seconds, they need playthings more substantial than a plastic hot dog that squeaks. Some owners actually give them bowling balls to play with, or automobile tires. You should probably keep these *outside.*

The AmStaff's phenomenal strength and indifference to physical pain also make careful training vitally important. This is the sort of dog who can take the shock from an "invisible fence" without so much as a whimper, and, if suitably aroused, pull so hard on its leash that it can knock its owner off her feet and drag her half a block. In such situations the last line of defense is the sure and certain knowledge that your AmStaff will obey the "sit" and

DOG TRAITS

WHO SHOULD GET THIS DOG?

These canines aren't for novice owners. Whoever acquires one should be willing to provide the tons of training and loving discipline AmStaffs need. Some owners swear these dogs are good with children, and indeed some are. But do you really want your kids' best buddy to be a bear-trap with legs? Get the family a Labrador retriever instead.

OWNER TRAITS

"stay" commands. So prepare to shell out money for those obedience classes (if you don't, you could wind up spending ten times as much for lawsuit settlements and attorney fees).

Special Perks: The AmStaff's coat is shorter than a Marine recruit's buzz cut, so grooming isn't a big issue. Also, most of the time they can be quite calm— almost lethargic. Sleeping and lying around the house suits them just fine.

Bugs in the System: These dogs are prone to skin troubles and allergies.

If someone broke into my house, this dog would: You know those companies the police use to clean up blood and body parts at particularly heinous crime scenes? You'll need one of those.

If you like American Staffordshire terriers, check out: The English Bulldog—it's a big, hulking dog with a teddy bear attitude. If you want a slightly smaller (and, perhaps, more manageable) version of the AmStaff, consider the Staffordshire bull terrier.

Weight: *30–35 pounds (13.5–15.8 kg).* *Height:* *17–20 inches (43.2–50.8 cm).* *Build:* *Stocky and sturdy.* *Coat:* *Coarse hair in blue or red, with markings of various colors.* *Brains:* *Extremely intelligent.* *Bladder Matters:* *No special house-training problems.*

The Incredible Origin: When nineteenth-century Australian cattlemen needed a dog to manage their unruly cows, they interbred various herding dogs with the native dingo to produce a hardy, strong canine that could bully bovines by biting at their backsides.

Trademark Traits: Like many herders, this can be a one-person dog. Though it craves its owner's attention, it doesn't need endless amounts of face time.

Headaches and Hassles: The breed is very strong willed and will try to dominate other dogs. Because its powerful jaws make it a very dangerous opponent, it should always be leashed in public. Also, it may apply its nearly overwhelming herding instinct to family members, nipping at their heels to get them to do what it wants. The cattle dog needs lots of exercise, including long walks and unleashed runs in a fenced area.

Special Perks: This breed is distinctive looking, to say the least. It's also totally loyal and (from a physical standpoint) very low maintenance. Cattle dogs are capable of learning complex tasks after only a few repetitions and of working with little or no super-vision. Perhaps because in the Outback, motivational Milk Bones and cries of "Good boy" were few and far between.

Bugs in the System: Though in general this breed is very healthy, some suffer from eye problems and/or hereditary deafness.

If someone broke into my house, this dog would: Herd him right back out again. The cattle dog isn't big on barking, but it is extremely courageous and very protective of its home, its family, and even other pets. And since its powerful bite was once enough to get the attention of thick-hided, half-wild cattle, you can imag-ine the effect it could have on a tender human posterior.

If you like the Australian cattle dog, check out: The Border collie. It's not as burly, but it's just as smart.

DOG TRAITS

WHO SHOULD GET THIS DOG?
A family or individual capable of providing the training and strong leadership this highly intelligent breed requires. Remember that an Australian cattle dog played Mad Max's sidekick in *The Road Warrior*, where it seemed quite contented amid the car chases, fights, and other post-apocalyptic mayhem.

OWNER TRAITS

Basenji

Weight: 21–24 pounds (9.5–10.8 kg). **Height:** *16–17 inches (40.6–43.2 cm).* **Build:** *Small but solidly built, with long legs.* **Coat:** *Very short hair in a variety of markings, from chestnut and white to black and white.* **Brains:** *Very intelligent, but they refuse to apply their intelligence to such human-friendly activities as learning tricks.* **Bladder Matters:** *No particular house-training issues.*

The Incredible Origin: Used in central Africa since time immemorial as a hunting and tracking dog, the basenji was introduced to the West in the mid-twentieth century. Interest in the breed was so high that when it was first shown at England's prestigious Crufts Show in 1937, security guards had to be called in to control the massive crowd. Its makeup is radically different from "conventional" dogs in that it cannot bark, it walks with a horse-like gait, and it cleans its fur by licking it like a cat. They are peerless hunters, able to track game by either scent or sight.

Trademark Traits: These dogs were only recently brought out of the bush, and it shows. Basenjis need a great deal of exercise; can be aggressive toward other dogs; will attack cats and other small animals; tend, if improperly socialized, to nip at children; and will bolt out a front door or unlatched gate if given the slightest opportunity. Basenjis love their masters, but they can display an almost catlike disregard for training—particularly to the "come" command. They must always be leashed in public. Often aloof, the basenji sleeps about 20 hours out of the day. But in the four hours it's awake, it's ready to rumble. This dog packs an energetic punch into its playtime.

Headaches and Hassles: The dog's clean habits and the fact that it can't bark have led some to call it a great apartment pet. Only if your apartment has foot-thick walls. The basenji can't bark, but it can howl—and even more horribly, serve up a bloodcurdling scream that aficionados compare to "the sound of a baby being murdered." Owners of scream-prone dogs have sometimes come home to find the police at their door. Basenjis raised in childless households may have trouble adjusting to a new baby. These dogs demand their owners' attention and can become petulant if their needs are denied. Regular exercise is needed to keep this breed on an even keel.

DOG TRAITS

WHO SHOULD GET THIS DOG?

Someone willing to deal with the special foibles of this most un-doglike dog. Remember that basenjis can be testy with kids, and that many aren't huge fans of cats, either.

OWNER TRAITS

Special Perks: Fans of this breed are enamored of its very un-doglike habits. Its foibles include furrowing its brow when on alert, producing an utterly human-looking expression of worry. And besides the screaming, the Basenji can make a wide range of other, less alarming sounds, including a trilling "yodel" that denotes happiness. They can also show unquestioning devotion and love toward their master. All in all, it's hard to imagine a more distinctive canine companion.

Bugs in the System: Susceptible to eye and hip problems, hemolytic anemia, and a disease called Fanconi syndrome. Some breeders claim that basenjis are "hypoallergenic" and thus good pets for allergy sufferers. Unfortunately, this isn't always the case. Some people are as violently allergic to them as they are to other dogs.

If someone broke into my house, this dog would: Have known well in advance that trouble was coming. Basenjis are very aware of their surroundings. Whether they would alert you to this development (remember, they don't bark) is in question.

If you like basenjis, check out: There is no other breed even remotely similar to the basenji.

Weight: 40–50 pounds (18.0–22.5 kg). *Height:* 13–15 inches (33.0–38.1 cm). *Build:* Extremely short legs supporting a long, stout body. Very heavy bones. *Coat:* Short hair, colored in some combination of black, white, and tan. *Brains:* The basset is a fairly intelligent animal, though its almost catlike disregard for authority has caused some to label it as "slow." *Bladder Matters:* Difficult to house-train. So difficult, in fact, that a small percentage never quite get the hang of it.

The Incredible Origin: Allegedly the basset (French for "low-set") started out as a hunting hound whose short legs allowed it to plow easily through underbrush. Examples were imported to America and England, where the variety seen today was perfected. The basset hound's sense of smell is said to be second only to that of the bloodhound, to which it is related.

Trademark Traits: Owners should get used to using the words "adorable" and "exasperating" in the same sentence. Bassets are utterly devoted to their families, wonderful with children, and so amusing that just watching one sprawled on its back, asleep, can provide hours of entertainment. Yet they can also be strong willed and highly resistant to training—including house-training. To get the dog to see things your way, be prepared to spend countless hours proffering treats and saying things like "Who's a good boy? *Bosley* is a good boy! Gooood boy!"

Headaches and Hassles: Like most hounds who formerly made their living tracking game, the basset is easily distracted by interesting odors—so easily that it must always be leashed in public, to keep it from wandering off. Also, these dogs only *look* like sedentary loafers. In fact they need plenty of exercise, or they tend to gain weight. Bassets *love* to eat. They will snatch food off counters and tables if given the opportunity and will tip over trash cans looking for scraps. Many users will purchase special extra-narrow food and water bowls so the basset won't drag its ears in its dinner. Some bassets drool so copiously that they can soak your pants if they rest their head on your leg. The drool issue can be particularly annoying at dinnertime, when a covetous

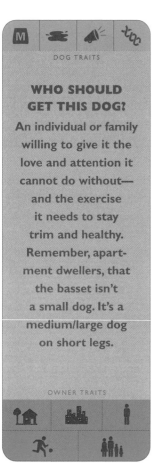

DOG TRAITS

WHO SHOULD GET THIS DOG?

An individual or family willing to give it the love and attention it cannot do without— and the exercise it needs to stay trim and healthy. Remember, apartment dwellers, that the basset isn't a small dog. It's a medium/large dog on short legs.

OWNER TRAITS

basset may forlornly watch you eat a steak while thick ropes of spittle slowly descend from the corners of its mouth to the floor. Even worse, it may shake its head and fling those ropes all over walls, furnishings, and you.

Special Perks: Pretty much everything a basset does is either amusing, photogenic, heartwarming, or all three. Its odd physique—long, low, wrinkly, droopy, yet strangely regal—only adds to its appeal. They can, if properly trained and socialized, be great friends to older, respectful children. Finally, it's worth repeating that the basset is more active than it looks. If you need an evening walking partner or dog park companion, this breed won't let you down.

Bugs in the System: The basset's torpedo-shaped frame makes it very adept at slipping its collar. Also, it is heir to a rather long list of genetic ailments, from skin conditions to benign tumors. Its floppy ears, if not regularly cleaned, can become infected or, at the very least, stinky.

If someone broke into my house, this dog would: Announce the arrival of a stranger with a bark or bloodcurdling howl. Otherwise, bassets aren't particularly good at home security.

If you like the basset hound, check out: The beagle. It's just as entertaining as the basset but without the drool.

Beagle

Weight: *26–33 pounds (11.7–14.9 kg).* **Height:** *13–16 inches (33.0–40.6 cm).* **Build:** *Compact and muscular.* **Coat:** *Smooth, short hair, in standard "hound" shades such as brown, black, and white.* **Brains:** *Highly intelligent and capable of prodigious feats of learning—provided that the curriculum interests them.* **Bladder Matters:** *Often difficult to house-train.*

The Incredible Origin: The breed, which was honed to its current form in England, has roots dating back to the Middle Ages. Designed primarily to find and flush hares, early varieties were allegedly small enough to fit in the pocket of a hunting jacket. These days only the larger version survives. In some corners of the world, even bigger "beagles" have been developed to track and tree big game animals, including leopards. They differ so greatly in size from the standard model that many are considered separate breeds.

Trademark Traits: In the old days canny hunters used this breed to chase game animals to exhaustion. Today, canny parents employ beagles to chase their *children* to exhaustion. Full of energy and endowed with an assertive, independent worldview (Snoopy, the libertine canine in the comic strip *Peanuts*, was a beagle), this dog will take whatever life gives it and come back for more. Remember, however, that it won't be content to exist on the periphery of your household, humbly lapping up whatever scraps of affection and attention you deign to give it. A beagle sees itself as a full-fledged member of the family and will demand to be treated as such.

Headaches and Hassles: The beagle is no lapdog. It can be energetic and feisty and needs regular exercise to stay healthy and trim. It can never go on a walk without a leash, because if it catches an interesting scent (and it's *always* catching interesting scents) it will leave you in the dust. Also, beagles can be tough to train. They respond to treats, praise, and absolutely nothing else. And speaking of treats, you might want to keep edible items well out of snatching distance and maybe put a lid on the kitchen trash can. Beagles love to eat and will "supplement their diets" (trans-

DOG TRAITS

WHO SHOULD GET THIS DOG?

An individual or family willing to give the beagle the exercise it needs and the training it requires. This dog is an excellent choice for the classic suburban family with kids—provided the family has a fenced yard and the time and inclination to satisfy a very people-oriented canine.

OWNER TRAITS

lation: steal food) if given half a chance.

Special Perks: As mentioned before, the beagle is a near-ideal companion and confidant for children. They make extremely energetic playmates. If they get dirty during all that goofing around, their short, tight coats are very easy to clean.

Bugs in the System: Beagles like to talk. Unfortunately, their version of "talking" consists of emitting a loud, bloodcurdling bark/howl called a "bay." They may do this while playing. Or on walks. Or when they pick up an interesting scent. Or when they've been left alone at home. Or for no discernible reason at all. It's advisable to experience the sound of a bay before opting for this breed. Also, the ears must be cleaned regularly to avoid infection.

If someone broke into my house, this dog would: Make a lot of noise. The typical beagle, if it detected an intruder, would greet it with a string of bays that would wake you, your neighbors, and probably the folks on the next block.

If you like beagles, check out: The basset hound, which offers all the traits of a hound in a more eye-catching (not to mention challenging) package. If you really want to go whole hog, investigate the king of the scent hunters, the bloodhound.

Weight: 40–55 pounds (18.0–24.8 kg). *Height:* 20–22 inches (50.8–55.9 cm). *Build:* Sturdy and strong. *Coat:* Long, coarse hair in a variety of shades. *Brains:* Intelligent, but like many herding dogs they are "independent thinkers." This is a code phrase that means "sometimes they just won't listen to you." Training can be a laborious process. *Bladder Matters:* House-training can take a while.

The Incredible Origin: Scotland could be called the unofficial herding capital of the world, based on the number of incredible herders (including the Border collie and collie) created there. The "beardie" is one of the lesser-known types. Resembling a midsized version of the Old English sheepdog, it is both a house pet and a working cattle and sheepdog.

Trademark Traits: The beardie's forlorn-looking gaze and somber expression belie its extroverted, energetic outlook. They can be somewhat stubborn, and like to be the center of attention. They can also be shy, unless carefully socialized when young.

Headaches and Hassles: An exuberant beardie can be too much for young children or the elderly. Also, this dog may try to "herd" family members by nipping at heels and backsides. They bark when they get excited—and often it doesn't take much to excite them. The beardie's coat must be carefully, laboriously groomed at home and undergo professional grooming also. None of this will keep this breed's long hair off your couch.

Special Perks: The beardie is an entertaining companion who loves to cut up for its family.

Bugs in the System: They can react badly to heartworm medication. Though generally healthy, some suffer from hip dysplasia, eye problems, hypothyroidism, and other conditions.

If someone broke into my house, this dog would: Raise the alarm. Like all herding dogs, the beardie is very conscious of its surroundings and suspicious of strangers.

If you like the bearded collie, check out: The briard, which sports pretty much the same haircut and attitude as the beardie, but runs 20 to 30 pounds (9–13.6 kg) larger.

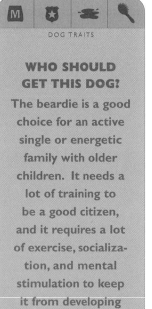

DOG TRAITS

WHO SHOULD GET THIS DOG?

The beardie is a good choice for an active single or energetic family with older children. It needs a lot of training to be a good citizen, and it requires a lot of exercise, socialization, and mental stimulation to keep it from developing bad habits. A fenced yard is a big, big plus.

OWNER TRAITS

Weight: 17–23 pounds (7.7–10.4 kg). *Height:* 15–17 inches (38.1–43.2 cm). *Build:* Lithe and muscular body. *Coat:* Thick, curly, wooly hair in liver, tan, sandy, and blue and tan. *Brains:* Bright, independent, and deserving of constant stimulation. *Bladder Matters:* No special house-training issues.

The Incredible Origin: Don't mistake the Bedlington for a prissy lapdog just because it has a fancy haircut. It was originally bred to hunt rats in English coal mines, then crossed with whippets to give it the speed to chase down larger game. Its hunting skills and small size made it a favorite with poachers.

Trademark Traits: The Bedlington is milder than the typical terrier, but also faster and even more athletic. It loves its family and plays well with children, but may not get along with unfamiliar dogs. That shouldn't be surprising, since this fuzzball was once used for pit fighting.

Headaches and Hassles: This dog has been afflicted with one of the goofiest haircuts ever perpetrated on a canine. It's complicated to do by yourself, expensive to *have* done, and, worst of all, it makes the poor Bedlington look like a nuclear-mutated lamb. Maybe the dog's funny looks make it angry. Bedlingtons can bark a lot and dig a lot, too. They will try to leap over or tunnel under fences. They will pursue small animals, are problematic around cats, and can't be trusted off their leash in public. Also, Bedlingtons require careful obedience training.

Special Perks: The Bedlington's haircut may be high mainte-nance, but the hair itself isn't. This dog sheds very little and doesn't have much of a "doggy" smell.

Bugs in the System: Prone to eye, liver, and kidney ailments.

If someone broke into my house, this dog would: Go into a high-pitched, machine-gun-like barking fit.

If you like the Bedlington terrier, check out: The miniature poodle, which can also be afflicted with embarrassing haircuts.

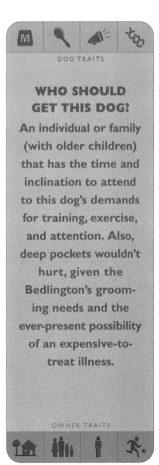

DOG TRAITS

WHO SHOULD GET THIS DOG?

An individual or family (with older children) that has the time and inclination to attend to this dog's demands for training, exercise, and attention. Also, deep pockets wouldn't hurt, given the Bedlington's groom-ing needs and the ever-present possibility of an expensive-to-treat illness.

OWNER TRAITS

*Weight: 70–115 pounds (31.5–51.8 kg). **Height:** 23–28 inches (58.4–69.9 cm). **Build:** Compact, muscular body. **Coat:** Long hair in a black, brownish-red, and white tricolor pattern. **Brains:** Bernese are of average to above-average intelligence, though they have been described as slow learners. Use only positive training techniques, because this dog can melt under criticism. **Bladder Matters:** No special house-training issues.*

The Incredible Origin: Originally one of several nondescript Swiss working dogs (it is named after the canton of Berne), the Bernese was on the verge of dying out when a group of interested breeders revived the line in the late nineteenth century. It was used as a general-purpose farm dog, and for pulling carts. Today it's a companion and show dog that can still, believe it or not, be used to pull carts.

DOG TRAITS

WHO SHOULD GET THIS DOG?

Preferably someone with deep pockets, because there's always the potential for hefty medical bills. Also, someone with experience handling plus-size canines. Young Bernese can be very excitable, making them poor choices for homes with elderly or very young members.

OWNER TRAITS

Trademark Traits: Well-trained adults are mellow, even-tempered dogs who always want to be with you, but not "in your face." Bernese can be a bit shy, which is why during their puppy-hood they should be exposed (in a pleasant way) to a wide range of people and situations. Their reaction to cats and other dogs can vary from indifference to hostility to an almost maternal interest, depending on the individual Bernese, and (perhaps more importantly) how well it was socialized.

Headaches and Hassles: These dogs like to dig. They also shed massively and require frequent brushing. In order to stay on an even keel, the typical Bernese needs lots of outdoor exercise (though during summer, excessive exertion can trigger heatstroke). However, it is not an outdoor dog. It wants to be near its family, and it can develop sometimes-severe behavioral problems if isolated or ignored.

Special Perks: A properly trained and socialized Bernese is good with children and very good at obedience training. Though they can be somewhat frenetic as puppies, after about two years they typically become calm, steady pets.

Bugs in the System: The average life span of a Bernese is a heartbreakingly short seven years. The breed is heir to a long, long list of genetic issues, including (but not confined to) cancer, hip and elbow dysplasia, autoimmune diseases, thyroid disorders, and a host of eye problems. A 2000 health study conducted by the Bernese Mountain Dog Club of America revealed that half the dogs who died during the program died of cancer. *Because of this dog's propensity for genetic disorders, acquiring a carefully bred dog from a responsible breeder is extremely important.* Obtaining such a pet-quality puppy can take more than a year and may cost as much as $1,000.

If someone broke into my house, this dog would: These canines weigh around 100 pounds (45.3 kg) and can be very protective of their families. You do the math.

If you like Bernese mountain dogs, check out: The Great Pyrenees and the Greater Swiss mountain dog, both of which are hulking specimens bred for mountain work.

Bichon Frise

Weight: *10–18 pounds (4.5–8.1 kg).* **Height:** *9–12 inches (22.9–30.5 cm).* **Build:** *A surprisingly sturdy, compact frame for such a small animal.* **Coat:** *Thick, white, curly, poodlelike fur.* **Brains:** *Capable of learning a full retinue of crowd-pleasing tricks.* **Bladder Matters:** *No special house-training difficulties.*

The Incredible Origin: This lovable lapdog's forebears (its close relatives include the Maltese and the nearly identical Bolognese) were favorites with Europe's elite for centuries. Startlingly bichon-like dogs show up repeatedly in Renaissance paintings, often attending French royalty or nestled in the arms of members of the Medici family. Masters ranging from Titian to Goya included them in their works. A handful of the dogs were brought back to the United States by soldiers at the close of World War I, but the breed didn't become established here until the middle of the twentieth century.

Trademark Traits: Loosely translated, bichon frise means "curly lapdog." That about sums this breed up. Its snow-white fur and near-human expression (not to mention its penchant for clowning around in nondestructive ways) make it an ideal apartment dog. The average bichon is good with children, tolerant of strangers, and gets along well with other dogs and noncanine pets. Most importantly, it likes nothing better than to spend hours snuggled up to its owner. This animal has been bred for centuries to be a pleasing household companion, and it shows.

Headaches and Hassles: Everything about the breed is low maintenance except for the hair. Its thick coat must be brushed regularly to prevent matting. If its hair is left au naturel, this dog looks like a scruffy little mutt (sorry, bichon fans). However, it can also be professionally clipped and fluffed into a breathtaking piece of canine topiary that would put the prissiest poodle to shame. It's up to you to choose which style to follow. Of course the dog itself couldn't care less if it looks like a dust mop or like something dipped out of a cotton-candy machine.

Special Perks: The bichon doesn't shed, so your $4,000 couch is safe. And this isn't the sort of canine that will regularly challenge

DOG TRAITS

WHO SHOULD GET THIS DOG?

The gentle, jovial bichon is ideal for singles, the elderly, and families with older, respectful children. Its small size and modest exercise needs make it perfect for almost any living arrangement. All it demands is attention—of which it will need quite a bit.

OWNER TRAITS

your authority, resist training, or develop "selective hearing" (that is, ignore you). The typical bichon is intelligent, eager to please, and (in most cases) more than happy to follow instructions. Also, these dogs are remarkably long-lived. The average life span is 15 to 16 years, but some approach and even surpass 20.

Bugs in the System: Some bichons are subject to allergies. Also their eyes tend to tear, creating discolored patches on their cheeks. This problem can be controlled with regular swabbing and cleaning (consult your veterinarian). The coat, if left natural, must be regularly combed and trimmed to prevent matting.

If someone broke into my house, this dog would: Bark and raise the alarm. For obvious reasons, the bichon can't take out a burglar single-handedly (unless the burglar is two feet tall).

If you like bichons, check out: The Maltese, a lapdog that many consider to be the kissing cousin of this elegant breed. Indeed, it was once called the bichon Maltese.

Weight: 90–110 pounds (40.5–49.5 kg). *Height:* 20–26 inches (50.8–66.0 cm). *Build:* Sturdy build, long ears and long nose. *Coat:* Short, most commonly in black and tan and liver and tan. *Brains:* The dog is of average intelligence. *Bladder Matters:* No special house-training difficulties.

The Incredible Origin: The bloodhound, allegedly developed in England in the late Middle Ages, descends in part from a now-extinct Belgian dog called the Saint Hubert. It has the most finely honed sense of smell of any dog.

Trademark Traits: Bloodhounds look scary in movies about prison escapes, but in real life they're as mellow and friendly as their droopy, forlorn facial expressions would lead you to believe. Which doesn't mean they can't be a handful. They can be resistant to training and tend to wander—especially if they pick up an interesting scent. And since their noses contain some 300 million scent-analyzing cells (about 100 million more than the typical dog), this can happen pretty regularly. Bloodhounds require a fenced yard and must always be leashed in public.

Headaches and Hassles: Bloodhounds emit a toe-curling howl that was once very useful in summoning hunters to their prey. You might consider it overkill when it is employed to, say, announce the arrival of the mail carrier. Also, these dogs drool during exercise (which they require regularly), snore incessantly, and can smell a bit gamy.

Special Perks: Their short coats are easy to maintain. Bloodhounds are also famously devoted to and tolerant of children.

Bugs in the System: Like many barrel-chested dogs, the bloodhound is susceptible to bloat. It can also suffer from stomach cramps, hip dysplasia, and ear infections.

If someone broke into my house, this dog would: The typical bloodhound never met a person it didn't like—even if that person is wearing a ski mask and brandishing a crowbar.

If you like bloodhounds, check out: If you're in the market for a big, snuffling hound, take a look at the basset.

DOG TRAITS

WHO SHOULD GET THIS DOG?

A family with older kids (and a large, fenced backyard) offers the ideal situation for this devoted companion. An active single would also be a good choice—especially if he or she wants a tireless (some might even say relentless) walking/jogging partner.

OWNER TRAITS

Weight: 30–50 pounds (13.5–22.5 kg). *Height:* 18–21 inches (45.7–53.3 cm). *Build:* Lithe, well-muscled body. *Coat:* Longish black-and-white hair. *Brains:* Startlingly intelligent and capable of learning the most complicated tricks. You probably knew guys in college who had less on the ball than the typical Border collie. *Bladder Matters:* No house-training problems.

The Incredible Origin: Versions of this dog have been chasing sheep along the Scottish/English frontier for centuries (hence its name). It is generally agreed to be the world's finest sheep-herder, capable of managing very large flocks with nothing but simple whistle commands from a shepherd. A pure working breed until very recently, it is now, for better or for worse, a popular pet and show dog.

Trademark Traits: Border collies are the type A's of the canine world. Full of intelligence and independence, they can be (depending almost entirely on your actions) either the best dog you've ever had or the worst. They are devoted to their owners but tend to ignore or be actively suspicious of strangers. They still have powerful herding instincts and must be carefully trained and socialized to prevent them from running off after small game or chasing cars.

Headaches and Hassles: Remember, this is no lapdog. You can see it in its laserlike stare. In Scotland, Australia, New Zealand, the United States, and elsewhere, this animal can still be found bounding through sodden pastures in all kinds of weather, bullying herds of sheep. In other words, this is a tough customer that is used to getting its way. A Border collie can (and will) push around a weak-willed owner. If it is ignored, it will also "make its own fun" by destroying household furnishings. Also, don't forget that this breed needs careful training, loving attention, exercise, and face time.

Special Perks: Earning the trust and loyalty of a Border collie is a truly wonderful thing—like becoming friends with the coolest

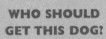

DOG TRAITS

WHO SHOULD GET THIS DOG?

This isn't a dog for amateurs. The Border collie needs a firm, loving master who can provide the ample training and attention necessary to get the most out of this exceptional breed. You must accept this dog as a part of the family—albeit a very tightly wrapped, high-strung part of the family.

OWNER TRAITS

person in your high school, or winning the approval of the only guy at the office whose opinion you respect. The fact that it will ignore every other person on the planet except you only adds to its cachet.

Bugs in the System: This dog's coat must be combed regularly and receive periodic professional grooming. Also, the typical owner may find the Border collie's prodigious intellect to be very much a double-edged sword. These animals must be extensively exercised and challenged mentally, or they can literally go buggy from boredom, manifesting obsessive-compulsive behaviors such as running endlessly in circles. Corporal punishment is a bad idea for any canine, but it can be particularly dicey with this breed. Border collies can react in bizarre, unexpected ways to punishment, displaying odd, seemingly nonsensical reactions to things such as shock collars and invisible fences, which can send some individuals into obsessive-compulsive frenzies.

If someone broke into my house, this dog would: Raise the alarm the minute anyone approached.

If you like Border collies, check out: The Shetland sheepdog (sheltie), a herding dog that enjoys the added advantage of looking like a miniature version of Lassie. However, it can be almost as twitchy as the Border collie.

Border Terrier

Weight: 11–16 pounds (5.0–7.2 kg). **Height:** 10 inches (25.4 cm). **Build:** Sturdy but graceful. **Coat:** Wiry hair, commonly in red or wheaten. **Brains:** Above average. These dogs are eager to please and easy to train. **Bladder Matters:** Takes rapidly and easily to house-training.

The Incredible Origin: Developed in the nineteenth century in the borderlands between Scotland and England, this nondescript, wirehaired, reddish-tan dog is perhaps the most utilitarian-looking of all terriers. Its thick, rough-looking double coat makes it impervious to weather, and it possesses the stamina to chase game for miles. You can see this toughness in the Border terrier's face, which wears a grim, perpetual "You talkin' to *me*?" expression. Though a recognized purebred, this scruffy-looking canine can easily be mistaken for a mutt.

Trademark Traits: This breed possesses all the vigor and in-your-face attitude one expects from terriers, though not in quite as big a dose as in such famous handfuls as Jack Russell terriers or fox terriers. Border terriers (unlike some other terrier varieties we could name) are usually less aggressive toward strange dogs, are less suspicious of visitors, and can even be somewhat laid-back (a phrase associated with terriers about as often as "model citizen" is with motorcycle gangs).

Headaches and Hassles: This dog likes to dig, so make sure it can't tunnel out of the backyard. Also, while it can usually get along with most felines (if careful introductions are made), it can never be trusted around such preylike species as rats, gerbils, or birds.

Special Perks: The Border terrier should be brushed weekly and professionally groomed perhaps twice a year, but that's about all. It sheds very little.

Bugs in the System: Some susceptibility to glaucoma. Otherwise, surprisingly free of genetic problems.

If someone broke into my house, this dog would: Raise a ruckus. With an alert, noisy Border terrier on patrol, no one's going to sneak into your bedroom unannounced.

If you like Border terriers, check out: The slightly larger and much redder Irish terrier.

DOG TRAITS

WHO SHOULD GET THIS DOG?

This wiry little canine can sometimes be a handful, but it still makes an excellent companion for families and singles who can learn to enjoy its sometimes-peppery personality and give it plenty of love, training, and attention. Older folks may also get a kick out of this attitude-filled dog.

OWNER TRAITS

Weight: *60–105 pounds (27.0–47.3 kg).* **Height:** *26–28 inches (66.0–71.1 cm).* **Build:** *Graceful but powerfully muscled, à la the greyhound.* **Coat:** *Long, silky hair in shades ranging from white to gray. Both solids and mixes are available.* **Brains:** *Highly intelligent and receptive to training—if it wishes to be.* **Bladder Matters:** *No particular house-training issues.*

The Incredible Origin: The borzoi (a.k.a. the Russian wolfhound) was developed in Russia to chase down and kill wolves. It could also hold its prey until a human hunter arrived to either dispatch or capture it. This dog (particularly the snow-white model) became a sought-after fashion accessory for both royalty and the rich throughout the world. Its loyal following included Queen Victoria. By the way, borzoi means "swift" in Russian.

Trademark Traits: Like the female assassins in James Bond movies, the borzoi is a disconcerting mix of beauty and lethality. More elegant and comely than even the collie (to which it was briefly interbred), it is also a peerless hunter. It can't be trusted around cats and other small animals and cannot be taken out unleashed in public. Plenty of clueless borzoi "enthusiasts" have acquired the dog solely for its looks, only to learn about its hunting prowess the hard way—such as when they came home to find the family cat dead in the living room. And in the dining room. And in the master bedroom . . .

Headaches and Hassles: This breed's hunting proclivity can't be overstated. If given half the chance, even the best-trained borzoi may bolt after a small, preylike animal—particularly if the animal in question happens to be running. However, in most cases properly socialized individuals can get along well with other dogs. Home life can also be somewhat problematic. They are devoted to their families and accept basic training, though most steadfastly refuse to "do tricks."

Be warned, however, that this breed won't take guff from people. Tug on their ears or play with them too roughly, and you're asking for a growl and, maybe, a nip. Given those facts, it should come as no surprise that borzois aren't good with young children.

DOG TRAITS

WHO SHOULD GET THIS DOG?

An experienced dog owner, preferably with a large, fenced yard. Some experts contend that borzois make acceptable apartment dogs, so long as they get regular, thorough exercise. This is a poor choice for the elderly (too big) and for families with young children.

OWNER TRAITS

They don't dislike kids, but they do dislike excessive noise, excessive attention, and excessive fooling around—which is pretty much what kids are all about.

Special Perks: Borzois need regular runs, but around the house they can be surprisingly placid. This isn't the sort of dog that will pester you constantly for belly rubs. Also, their silky coats usually require nothing more complicated than regular brushing. These tireless runners are excellent jogging partners—so long as they are kept leashed and the weather isn't too warm.

Bugs in the System: Prone to bloat. Leg fractures can also be a problem.

If someone broke into my house, this dog would: Either stand by or wade in, depending on the nature of the individual dog in question. The borzoi isn't a very good watchdog because it doesn't bark all that much. However, many still possess a very strong prey drive, and they don't take kindly to strangers who threaten their "people." If such a situation arises, this type of borzoi will end the encounter in seconds with its powerful jaws and lightning speed.

If you like the borzoi, check out: The greyhound, which also looks quite elegant but is much, much easier to groom. Or, if long hair is your thing, investigate the lavishly-maned Afghan hound.

Boston Terrier

Weight: 17–25 pounds (7.7–11.3 kg). *Height:* 15–17 inches (38.1–43.2 cm). *Build:* Slight, almost fragile-looking frame. *Coat:* Short, white and black hair. Brindle and black and brindle and white are also available. *Brains:* Average intelligence. *Bladder Matters:* No special house-training problems.

The Incredible Origin: The Boston terrier was, apparently, actually developed in the city of Boston. During the nineteenth century an English terrier and an English bulldog were crossed to create the prototype canine, which was refined in subsequent pairings to the form we know today.

Trademark Traits: This breed has some unusual traits—unusual for a terrier, that is. In general they are less excitable, more well behaved, and less of an all-around pain in the butt than, say, a cairn. Or a Jack Russell. Or an Airedale. Or (insert name of pretty much any other terrier on the planet here). Perhaps this is because the placid bulldog aspect of its personality dominates—or that, unlike its relatives, most of whom were bred to hunt and kill something (usually a whole lot of somethings), this terrier was never meant to be anything but a companion.

Headaches and Hassles: Bostons aren't quite as wired as other terriers, but they can still be a handful. They may nip younger children. They also tend to drool when excited.

Special Perks: The Boston's placid, mostly amiable personality has won it the nickname "the American gentleman."

Bugs in the System: Boston terriers shouldn't exercise heavily on hot days, because they are prone to heatstroke. Also, this breed doesn't come by its pointy ears naturally. It is born with floppy ears that must then be surgically cropped. This is done purely for aesthetics. In many places around the world, this operation is considered animal cruelty and is illegal.

If someone broke into my house, this dog would: Bark. Boston terriers are very, very keen on barking.

If you like Boston terriers, check out: The pug, which offers roughly the same look as the Boston, but even less attitude.

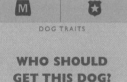

DOG TRAITS

WHO SHOULD GET THIS DOG?

The Boston is equally at home in an apartment or suburban home, with a family or an individual—provided it gets plenty of love and attention. However, because of its size and relative fragility, it is a particularly bad choice for homes with very young children.

OWNER TRAITS

*Weight: 60–90 pounds (27.0–40.5 kg). **Height:** 23–27 inches (58.4–68.6 cm). **Build:** Well-muscled and broad-backed. **Coat:** Long, very dense black hair. **Brains:** Highly intelligent and capable of tackling complex training. **Bladder Matters:** No special house-training problems.*

The Incredible Origin: The breed was developed to herd cattle in Flanders, the border region between the Netherlands and France (hence its decidedly unromantic but very descriptive name, which means "cowherd from Flanders"). It proved to be such a useful war dog, doing everything from acting as a courier to seeking out the wounded in no man's land, that it was nearly wiped out in World War I—and again in World War II.

Trademark Traits: Like most guarding/herding types, the Bouvier never met a stranger it didn't distrust. But though stand-offish with new people and often actively belligerent to unknown dogs, it displays unswerving loyalty to its owner.

Headaches and Hassles: The Bouvier needs professional groom-ing to maintain its rough-looking coat. Miss a couple of salon appointments and this dog will look like a knot of hair fished out of a shower drain. Also, the Bouvier's pointy ears are created through surgery. If left alone, they're disarmingly floppy.

Special Perks: The adult Bouvier is nearly tireless, making it an excellent cool-weather jogging partner.

Bugs in the System: Other than hip dysplasia and eye problems (such as cataracts), it has few genetic illnesses.

If someone broke into my house, this dog would: Very quickly become attached to the unannounced guest—and by "become attached" we mean "sink its teeth into one of his extremities and refuse to let go."

If you like the Bouvier, check out: The Kerry blue terrier, fea-turing the same curly hair and protect-the-family-at-all-costs attitude as the Bouvier, but in a slightly smaller package.

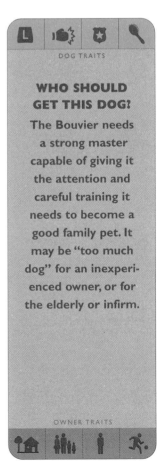

DOG TRAITS

WHO SHOULD GET THIS DOG?
The Bouvier needs a strong master capable of giving it the attention and careful training it needs to become a good family pet. It may be "too much dog" for an inexperi-enced owner, or for the elderly or infirm.

OWNER TRAITS

Boxer

Weight: *55–70 pounds (24.8–31.5 kg).* **Height:** *21–25 inches (53.3–63.5 cm).* **Build:** *Graceful, athletic-looking frame with well-defined muscles.* **Coat:** *Extremely short hair in various shades of brindle and various color combinations including red, white, and light yellow.* **Brains:** *The boxer can display above-average intelligence, though some resist training.* **Bladder Matters:** *No particular house-training problems.*

DOG TRAITS

WHO SHOULD GET THIS DOG?

Ideally, the boxer needs a fenced yard, older children with which to play, and a master who can give it the training and attention it requires to thrive. However, it can also make a good companion for an attentive single—provided he or she doesn't take it on long jogs during heat waves.

OWNER TRAITS

The Incredible Origin: The breed was developed in nineteenth-century Germany, where it was used for everything from hunting to pit fighting to cart pulling. It was introduced to America in a big way at the end of World War II. Today's version is something of an oddity—a powerful, scary-looking guardian that's infused with a goofy, play-all-day attitude reminiscent of that of a golden retriever. Its celebrity owners include (perhaps inevitably) Sylvester Stallone. Which brings up an important point: If you acquire a boxer, please resist the temptation to name it after a famous pugilist. At first blush calling it Rocky or Cassius may seem clever and original, but it's not. It seems as if every male owner of this breed falls into this name trap, which is why you'll sometimes witness the sad spectacle of two men at the dog park shouting "Tyson! Here, Tyson!" to attract different boxers.

Trademark Traits: Talk about not being able to tell a book by its cover. One look at the boxer's well-muscled body and glowering expression leaves no doubt as to what it was made for. But while they are indeed strong, agile, and somewhat protective of their owners, they also possess a jolly, fun-loving streak. It takes very little (a treat, the sudden arrival of an expected guest, the sudden arrival of a *stranger*) to send a boxer into paroxysms of prancing, butt-wagging joy.

Headaches and Hassles: Boxers are vulnerable to both excessive heat and (in part because of their very short coats) to cold. They must receive careful socialization and training at an early age to control their boisterous physicality (they are famed leapers, as many an owner carrying a sandwich through the house has learned) and their tendency to try to dominate a weak owner.

Some drool, and many snore. Their ears are naturally floppy. They must be surgically altered to make them pointy.

Special Perks: The typical boxer may retain its physical prowess well into old age, running and jumping years after dogs of similar ages have retired to the rug in front of the fireplace. It is also devoted to its family and is a particular friend to children, whom it will zealously (but usually not overzealously) protect. However, they can be too rambunctious for toddlers and very young children. Its short coat requires minimal care.

Bugs in the System: Because their short snouts compromise their breathing, boxers are susceptible to heat exhaustion. They can also suffer hip dysplasia, epilepsy, tumors (both benign and malignant), allergies, and heart problems, including cardiomyopathy. All-white boxers should be tested for deafness.

If someone broke into my house, this dog would: Likely give the unannounced visitor the benefit of the doubt. Boxers are good guardians, but they don't subscribe to the Dirty Harry–like, "Go ahead, make my day," mentality one can see in other guarding breeds.

If you like boxers, check out: The English bulldog, which can be quite playful, but not as in-your-face.

Weight: 25–50 pounds (11.3–22.5 kg). *Height:* 16–20 inches (40.6–50.8 cm). *Build:* Muscular and compact. *Coat:* The breed comes in flat, wavy, and curly coats. *Brains:* Above-average intelligence, with a docile temperament perfect for training—provided the lessons are offered in an upbeat manner. *Bladder Matters:* No special house-training issues.

The Incredible Origin: This dog certainly doesn't put on airs. The line allegedly arose from a single stray found loitering outside a church in Spartanburg, South Carolina. A parishioner took it home, named it Dumpy, and discovered during hunting expeditions that it was an outstanding retriever. A trainer, Whitaker Boykin, crossed Dumpy with other hunting dogs, producing the modern Boykin. Nowadays, it is the state dog of South Carolina.

Trademark Traits: Friendly and inquisitive, energetic and enthusiastic. The Boykin loves people and is a particular friend to older, respectful children.

Headaches and Hassles: The long coat is prone to matting and needs weekly (at least) brushing. The Boykin tends to put on weight and should receive daily exercise to stay trim. Some Boykins can be very, very hyper. The best approach is to check if the problem exists in your dog's bloodline.

Special Perks: The dog has great hot-weather stamina and is a very strong swimmer.

Bugs in the System: Problems include hip dysplasia, eye disorders, and skin allergies. Some poorly bred Boykins can show undue, unprovoked aggression.

If someone broke into my house, this dog would: Do little if anything. Unfortunately, the Boykin is a lousy watchdog.

If you like the Boykin spaniel, check out: The much more common cocker spaniel.

DOG TRAITS

WHO SHOULD GET THIS DOG?

Families and individuals interested in a lively, humorous dog, and who are willing to provide the exercise, training, and face time it requires. Older children would be a definite plus for this gregarious canine.

OWNER TRAITS

Weight: 65–80 pounds (29.3–36.0 kg). *Height:* 21–27 inches (53.3–68.6 cm). *Build:* Solidly built. *Coat:* Long, thick, stiff coat in all solid colors, except white. *Brains:* Very intelligent and amenable to gentle training. *Bladder Matters:* No special house-training problems.

The Incredible Origin: This French sheepdog is famous for its energy and intelligence. It's been used as everything from a guide dog to a war dog. During World War I it patrolled no man's land looking for wounded soldiers who could still be saved. It was so good at triage that the legend arose that if you were lying on the battlefield and a briard passed you by, you were a goner.

Trademark Traits: Friendly and smart, but not as wired as some other herding dogs, such as the Border collie or sheltie. They are gentle with and protective of children—so much so that they have been known to intervene if "their" kids get a spanking.

Headaches and Hassles: Its long, coarse coat requires lots of combing. Get used to the idea of seeing this hair on your living room furnishings.

Special Perks: The briard is somewhat distant to strangers, but not paranoid. It loves its family and close friends and has few personality or emotional tics. Also, its coat is said to repel moisture and mud—to a degree.

Bugs in the System: Briards are subject to bloat.

If someone broke into my house, this dog would: Defend its loved ones to the bitter end. The briard may look like a shaggy goofball, but it comes from a long line of legendary guardians. In France they were sometimes called "doormat dogs," after their habit of controlling the front door by plopping down in front of it and going to sleep.

If you like the briard, check out: The bearded collie—a herding dog with a worldview similar to that of the briard, but a body almost half its size.

DOG TRAITS

WHO SHOULD GET THIS DOG?

This is an excellent family dog, provided the family can meet the briard's fairly heavy demands for exercise and mental stimulation. The dog is also a good choice for a young, attentive, active single. A well-conditioned briard can match even the most dedicated jogger.

OWNER TRAITS

Brittany (Spaniel)

Weight: 28–33 pounds (12.6–14.9 kg). *Height:* 17–21 inches (43.2–52.1 cm). *Build:* Graceful, athletic-looking. *Coat:* Dense, flat, wavy hair in various combinations of white with orange, brown, black, or liver. Also in tricolor or roan. *Brains:* Brittanys are capable of handling extensive training, but they can be stubborn and a bit sulky. The best approach is never to punish. Simply reward good behavior and ignore unwanted behavior. *Bladder Matters:* No special house-training problems.

The Incredible Origin: Developed in France, the Brittany was refined by nineteenth-century breeders into today's canine—an excellent bird dog that can both point and retrieve and that possesses an uncanny sense of smell. Its friendly demeanor also makes it a good family dog.

Trademark Traits: Exuberant and energetic, the Brittany is always ready for a game of fetch or a romp around the yard. They are also good with children, other pets, even complete strangers. Some, however, may have a problem with cats, squirrels, and other small animals.

Headaches and Hassles: Brittanys don't like to be left alone for long stretches. If they *are* left alone, they may find ways to register their displeasure—ways that involve property damage. Brittanys need exercise every day and can become a bit buggy if you shortchange them.

Special Perks: When it comes to dogs that love their families, the Brittany is right up there with such favorites as the golden retriever and the Labrador retriever.

Bugs in the System: The Brittany is a healthy breed, though epilepsy and hip dysplasia are occasionally seen. The ears should be checked for infection and cleaned regularly.

If someone broke into my house, this dog would: Bark to announce the stranger's approach. But once the intruder was actually *in* the house, the agreeable dog would probably give him a tour.

If you like Brittany spaniels, check out: The Boykin spaniel and cocker spaniel.

DOG TRAITS

WHO SHOULD GET THIS DOG?
Someone who's interested in acquiring a family member, rather than a pet. The Brittany will want to participate in every part of your life. In exchange, you'll get a loyal, loving companion and, if you have children, a devoted friend to them.

OWNER TRAITS

Brussels Griffon

*Weight: 6–9 pounds (2.7–4.1 kg). **Height:** 9–11 inches (22.9–27.9 cm). **Build:** Tiny but sturdy. **Coat:** Long and wiry or short and wiry, depending on the type. Color combinations can include shades such as black, tan, and red. **Brains:** Reasonably intelligent, but somewhat difficult to train. **Bladder Matters:** Some griffons can never be reliably house-trained.*

The Incredible Origin: Controversy rages over just what a Brussels griffon actually is. The little monkey-faced dogs were originally bred as ratters, and they are so similar to two other breeds, the Belgian griffon and the Petit Brabançon, that all three are often lumped together. Adding to the confusion, some experts contend that another monkey-faced dog, the German-born affenpinscher (see page 32), was brought in after World War II to reinvigorate the decimated griffon population. Yet other breeders (*Belgian* breeders) claim it was the other way around.

Trademark Traits: The big selling point of these tiny canines is that they all look like heavily bearded, grumpy little men. They are inquisitive and at times somewhat hot tempered.

Headaches and Hassles: Griffons like children about as much as W. C. Fields did. But at least Fields never bit one—which griffons have been known to do. These dogs tend to be shy, so it doesn't take more than a couple of bad experiences (such as rough handling) to turn them into basket-case recluses.

Special Perks: This is a unique little dog. A walk around the block and a frolic in the living room is all the exercise it requires.

Bugs in the System: Griffons don't reproduce easily or often. Puppies are delivered by Cesarean section, and they are extremely fragile during their first weeks. Adding to the breed's troubles is the fact that one was featured in the movie *As Good As It Gets*, creating a demand for puppies among usually unqualified novices.

If someone broke into my house, this dog would: Bark. Probably. Hopefully.

If you like the Brussels griffon, check out: That other short-faced, angry-looking little dog, the affenpinscher.

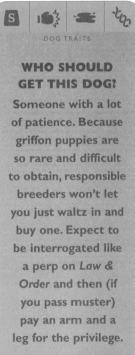

DOG TRAITS

WHO SHOULD GET THIS DOG?
Someone with a lot of patience. Because griffon puppies are so rare and difficult to obtain, responsible breeders won't let you just waltz in and buy one. Expect to be interrogated like a perp on *Law & Order* and then (if you pass muster) pay an arm and a leg for the privilege.

OWNER TRAITS

Bulldog (English)

Weight: *40–50 pounds (18.0–22.5 kg).* **Height:** *12–16 inches (30.5–40.6 cm).* **Build:** *Solid, stocky body on short legs.* **Coat:** *Short and smooth hair, in colors ranging from red to white to various brindles.* **Brains:** *Average intelligence.* **Bladder Matters:** *House-training can sometimes be a drawn-out affair.*

The Incredible Origin: The British have kept "bull dogs" for centuries, but they bore scant resemblance to the modern version. In the old days the dogs were bred to actually fight bulls, so they had smaller heads, more athletic bodies, and a much more bloody-minded worldview. When bullbaiting was banned in the nineteenth century, this canine became a dog show staple—after some drastic selective breeding that did away with its violent nature and reshaped it into the stout, dour-looking, big-headed palooka we have today.

Trademark Traits: The bulldog, along with the Newfoundland, belongs to a very select fraternity—the brotherhood of dangerous-looking dogs that aren't really dangerous. This canine wants to be your buddy. Heck, it wants to be *everybody's* buddy. It's remarkably loving with its family, tolerant of strangers, and reasonably amenable to training.

Headaches and Hassles: A bulldog can be surprisingly delicate for such a burly-looking breed. It needs exercise but can't tolerate long walks in hot weather, which very quickly can lead to heat exhaustion. Bulldogs are also, for the most part, terrible swimmers and can drown in deep (and even not-so-deep) water. Some drool, and all snore. A bulldog tends to chew on things if it becomes bored or lonely. Give it plenty of toys (tough ones that it can't gnaw apart and swallow) so it will lay off your shoes and home furnishings. And consider getting it a companion—say, an altered (spayed/neutered) bulldog of the opposite sex.

Special Perks: The bulldog is very laid-back, making it an ideal companion for couch potatoes. While in many cases its physical limitations make it impossible for bulldogs to serve as reliable playmates for children, the breed is nevertheless extremely tolerant

DOG TRAITS

WHO SHOULD GET THIS DOG?

A family or individual interested in a very scary-looking, but mellow-acting, pet. Also, someone willing (and financially able) to provide the bulldog the special medical attention it may require. This breed's relatively low activity level makes it a worthy candidate for apartment living.

OWNER TRAITS

of their presence and antics. The only "aggressive" thing it would ever do is exuberantly knock someone over by jumping on them.

Bugs in the System: Hereditary health problems include hip dysplasia, plus a long list of complaints associated with the breed's pushed-in face, including (but not confined to) narrow nostrils, eye problems, and dangerously narrow tracheas. Also, bulldog pregnancies can be very tricky. Puppies must often be delivered by Cesarean section, because their heads are too big to pass through the birth canal. Because of this, you may have to wait as long as a year to acquire a carefully bred puppy. Caring for these dogs can be such a complicated matter that it's worth seeking out a veterinarian experienced with the breed.

If someone broke into my house, this dog would: Deter most troublemakers with its looks. If the mere sight *isn't* enough, the typical bulldog, if pushed to the wall, may take action. But don't count on it.

If you like the English bulldog, check out: The powerful bull terrier, a member of the brotherhood of dangerous-looking dogs that, when the chips are down, will actually come out swinging. Or the French bulldog, which both looks and *is* utterly harmless.

Bulldog (French)

Weight: 22–28 pounds (9.9–12.6 kg). *Height:* Up to 12 inches (30.5 cm). *Build:* Sturdy, compact body. *Coat:* Short, soft fur, in a variety of shades. *Brains:* Reasonably intelligent, though it may try to resist (or ignore) training. *Bladder Matters:* House-training can be somewhat protracted.

The Incredible Origin: The ancestry of this breed is the sort of thing dog enthusiasts like to debate at great length on Sunday afternoons, after they've had a few wine spritzers. The French, inevitably, say its creation was an entirely Gaulish affair. The English, however, assert that it was produced by breeding French stock to runty English bulldogs, creating the smallish French version.

Trademark Traits: The "Frenchie" would be in big trouble if it ever got in a pit with a bull. The French bulldog prefers less intense activities, such as cuddling on the couch with its master and frolicking with children. However, it still carries a streak of fearlessness and will challenge strange dogs many times its size. So keep it on a leash in public.

Headaches and Hassles: Hope you like listening to snoring. Also, you might want to hold off on over-the-counter dog biscuits. Wheat gives some Frenchies the toots.

Special Perks: The Frenchie loves people, usually doesn't bark excessively, has an easy-to-maintain coat, and can be exercised with short walks and living room romps.

Bugs in the System: The breed is subject to heatstroke if exercised too much in hot weather. It can also have eye problems. As with other large-headed breeds, such as the English bulldog, its puppies must often be delivered by Cesarean section.

If someone broke into my house, this dog would: Bark a great deal. These dogs can be quite territorial, and they hate it when people drop in unannounced.

If you like the French bulldog, check out: The pug, for a more compact take on bug-eyed, snoring canines. Or the English bulldog, which is as friendly as the Frenchie, but more serious-looking.

DOG TRAITS

WHO SHOULD GET THIS DOG?

The French bulldog fits in with almost anyone and with almost any living arrangement. All that's required is that you give this compact canine companion careful training and plenty of affection.

OWNER TRAITS

*Weight: 100–130 pounds (45.0–58.5 kg). **Height:** 24–27 inches (61.0–68.6 cm). **Build:** Muscular and massive. **Coat:** Very short hair in solid red, fawn, or brindle, with a black muzzle and black around the eyes. **Brains:** Requires lifetime obedience training. Bullmastiffs can sometimes be resistant and stubborn, which means you have to be equally persistent and strong. **Bladder Matters:** No special house-training problems.*

The Incredible Origin: In nineteenth-century England, gamekeepers needed some serious muscle to help them deal with poachers. So they crossed the English bulldog with the gigantic mastiff, creating a dog that was not only enormous, but also fast and canny enough to sneak up on the bad guys. Interestingly, instead of turning its victims into hash, the typical bullmastiff would simply knock them flat and hold them in place for its master.

Trademark Traits: For a guard dog, the bullmastiff can be surprisingly laid-back. But then, what does such a huge, strong animal have to prove? This doesn't mean, however, that it doesn't need training. Even a benign bullmastiff can cause a great deal of trouble if you can't properly control it. One that has an aggressive streak can be a king-size problem.

Headaches and Hassles: Bullmastiffs ooze drool by the quart. Experienced owners know to keep "drool rags" (typically cloth diapers) handy. Some Web sites even sell special monogrammed versions. This dog also sheds constantly, and its short hair is particularly hard to remove from clothing and furnishings. Young bullmastiffs are large and energetic, which doesn't bode well for fragile coffee-table knickknacks, unsteady toddlers, or infirm elderly people. They may also "slime" the unsuspecting by mouthing their extremities. And speaking of mouths, the typical bullmastiff Hoovers four cups of high-quality food down its piehole daily. Another thing to consider: You'll need to "poop scoop" your yard regularly. When one of these dogs starts unloading on your lawn, every day is Hell's Easter Egg Hunt.

Special Perks: If you can get past the drool, a well-trained, well-

DOG TRAITS

WHO SHOULD GET THIS DOG?

This breed is strictly for experienced, physically and mentally strong owners with the time and inclination to properly train and socialize it. Owning a large, fenced yard wouldn't hurt, either. The bullmastiff is way too big for the elderly or for families with very young children.

OWNER TRAITS

socialized bullmastiff is a wonderful and genuinely lovable dog. Its loose hair blends nicely with khaki pants and camel-colored coats and sweaters.

Bugs in the System: The bullmastiff, like all gigantic breeds, suffers for its size. Don't overexert them in extreme heat (they can succumb to heatstroke) and don't leave them out in the cold. Their coat is too short to insulate against the elements. As for medical issues, they are heir to a range of eye problems, to bloat, and to hip dysplasia.

If someone broke into my house, this dog would: Be a peerless bodyguard but an indifferent property guard. If someone breaks in while you're home, the bullmastiff will likely toss the intruder to the ground like a rag doll and (in a holdover from its days of hunting poachers), restrain him until backup arrives. If someone breaks in when you *aren't* home, the bullmastiff may react, or it may not. It's worried about *you*, not your DVD collection.

If you like the bullmastiff, check out: The mastiff, if you want a really, *really* big dog. Or the boxer, if you'd like a similar design in a smaller, less spit-soaked package.

*Weight: 45–65 pounds (20.3–29.3 kg). **Height:** 12–18 inches (30.5–45.7 cm). **Build:** Very solid, muscular body with short legs and a long, wide muzzle. **Coat:** Extremely short hair, either solid white or with spots. **Brains:** Above-average intelligence. This is good during training, bad when applied to mischief. **Bladder Matters:** No special house-training difficulties, though a bored or ignored bull terrier may register its displeasure by laying down a new pattern on your entryway rug.*

The Incredible Origin: This breed was allegedly developed in nineteenth-century England for pit fighting. However, its unorthodox looks made it a popular companion dog—after decades of selective breeding diluted its killer instinct. Today's version could still shred pretty much anyone or anything it wished. It just doesn't wish to. Most of the time.

Trademark Traits: One of this breed's most endearing traits is that while it looks like a killing machine, the typical, well-bred, well-socialized "bullie" is a goofball at heart. If raised and socialized with children, they can make excellent, near-tireless playmates and protectors. This breed wants to be involved at all times with its owners, and it doesn't take well to being ignored or left alone for extended periods. In order to be all it can be, it must be carefully trained.

Headaches and Hassles: Bull terriers will pursue small animals, so they can never be taken out in public unleashed. Likewise, they can be problematic around cats, unless they are introduced to them at a young age. And while they usually won't start fights with unfamiliar dogs, they will quickly finish them. Always remember that bull terriers can be very protective. If your kid gets pushed around by a bully, your four-legged bullie might retaliate in a very definitive—and legally actionable—way.

Special Perks: In spite of their athletic builds, bull terriers don't demand endless exercise. Regular walks will suffice. In exchange you get a distinctive-looking, happy dog that's devoted to you and yours—plus a very effective personal protection system.

DOG TRAITS

WHO SHOULD GET THIS DOG?
Previous owners include General George S. Patton and President Teddy Roosevelt, though you needn't be a military or political official to get one. The ideal owner is a family or individual willing to provide the leadership, training, and attention necessary to keep this exuberant animal on an even keel.

OWNER TRAITS

Bugs in the System: Roughhousing should be strictly controlled during puppyhood, because too much activity can injure this breed's rapidly developing joints. There is some deafness among pure-white bull terriers, but in general the breed is quite healthy. It's important to remember that this dog is very, very strong for its size. Freakishly strong. Incredible Hulk strong. These canines are built like linebackers and, unless instructed otherwise, tend to play rough. They can merrily deal out head butts, mow people down with shots from their meaty shoulders, and use other such tactics rarely seen outside of professional wrestling. It makes an excellent playmate for older kids but not for toddlers. And here's another good reason to make sure yours is carefully trained. If an overexuberant bull terrier starts tugging at its leash, there's precious little you can do to stop it.

If someone broke into my house, this dog would: Defend you and yours, no matter the odds. The mere sight of an enraged bull terrier is enough to make almost anyone turn tail. If that doesn't work, having a huge chunk of flesh ripped from their thigh almost certainly will.

If you like bull terriers, check out: The bull terrier (miniature) for basically the same animal in a more convenient size.

*Weight: 20 pounds (9.0 kg). **Height:** 14 inches (35.6 cm). **Build:** Very powerful (like the standard-sized bull terrier, but smaller). **Coat:** Extremely short hair. **Brains:** Above-average intelligence—which means they need careful training to keep them from using their smarts for nefarious purposes. **Bladder Matters:** No special house-training problems.*

The Incredible Origin: Bred mostly from undersized standard bull terriers, this dog is basically a one-third-scale replica of the full-size "bullie."

Trademark Traits: As with its bigger relative, the miniature possesses an exuberant, happy-go-lucky attitude. Like Dennis the Menace, these curious canines are forever getting into things, playing with toys, and looking for adventure.

Headaches and Hassles: This breed needs company. If you leave them alone all day, particularly when they're puppies, you're practically guaranteeing that they will develop antisocial personality tics, such as housebreaking problems, excessive barking, and a tendency toward property damage. Also, male bullies don't get along with other male dogs.

Special Perks: All the fun of a bull terrier but in a more convenient package. Parents who want a full-size bullie but worry that it will knock their kids down like bowling pins may find this version more acceptable. Be warned, however, that these pint-size versions still enjoy rough play.

Bugs in the System: Miniatures can suffer from eye and heart defects.

If someone broke into my house, this dog would: Probably inflict severe ankle and below-the-knee flesh wounds.

If you like the miniature bull terrier, check out: The French bulldog, a far less pugnacious creature than the typical bull terrier. Or opt for the full-size bull terrier, which is literally twice the dog of the miniature.

DOG TRAITS

WHO SHOULD GET THIS DOG?
A family or individual who won't leave it alone all hours of the day. Miniature bull terriers need to be part of their family's lives. If they feel excluded, they may cause trouble. If they *don't* feel excluded, they can fit in with families, singles, even retirees.

OWNER TRAITS

Weight: 14–16 pounds (6.3–7.2 kg). Height: 11–12 inches (27.9–30.5 cm). Build: Compact, powerful body. Very strong for its size. Coat: Coarse, longish hair in a range of shades from cream to gray to black. Brains: Extremely intelligent and receptive to training. Unfortunately, a bored cairn may use its smarts to, say, redecorate your living room in shabby chic—minus the chic. Bladder Matters: No special house-training problems.

The Incredible Origin: Developed in Scotland and named after the loose piles of stones, called cairns, used there to mark graves and property lines, this dog is one of a slew of lethal little terriers (including the Jack Russell, Norwich, and West Highland) bred to chase, corner, and pound the snot out of everything from rats to foxes.

Trademark Traits: Like most terriers, the cairn is fearless, impervious to pain and fatigue, and full of energy.

Headaches and Hassles: Even the most carefully trained cairn can never, ever be trusted off its leash in public. As if fueled by Red Bull and Caramel Macchiatos, cairns will race across busy streets, charge out of fenced yards, and leave angry owners in the dust as they pursue potential game.

Special Perks: The cairn is absolutely devoted to its master, sometimes to the point of jealousy. Though it's problematic with other animals, it enjoys the company of human strangers (once they are properly introduced). Its perennial expression, a mix of happiness and mischief, perfectly sums up its character.

Bugs in the System: Their coarse, long hair is prone to matting and must be brushed regularly. Some owners prefer a shaggy natural look—even though a cairn in all its hirsute glory resembles Rod Stewart's coiffure atop four short, furry legs. If such imagery disturbs you, cairns can be given a closer trim, to no ill effect.

If someone broke into my house, this dog would: A savvy cairn will detect potential trouble and raise the alarm long before an intruder can get anywhere near your door or window.

If you like cairn terriers, check out: The Norwich and Norfolk terriers, which are descended from this breed, as is the West Highland white terrier.

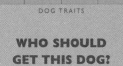

DOG TRAITS

WHO SHOULD GET THIS DOG?

A family or individual who's willing to channel this breed's enthusiasm into regular play and careful training sessions. Also, someone who doesn't mind a dog that will unexpectedly leap onto his or her lap and deliver ten or twelve chin-to-forehead licks. Which cairns will do. Repeatedly.

OWNER TRAITS

Weight: 10–18 pounds (4.5–8.1 kg). Height: 12–13 inches (30.5–33.0 cm). Build: Short and compact. Coat: Long, silky hair in red and white, ruby, tricolor, or black and tan. Brains: Easy to train. Bladder Matters: No special house-training problems.

The Incredible Origin: This little dog with the big name is a twentieth-century reconstruction of the toy spaniels that were popular pets for British royalty from the seventeenth to nineteenth centuries. It is currently the most popular toy breed in England.

Trademark Traits: The cavalier is a social butterfly that thrives on the companionship of its family. Its merry expression and happy (but not hyper) outlook make it a wonderful pet.

Headaches and Hassles: Cavaliers may be lapdogs, but they have hunting roots—which means they tend to chase things. They will even go after cars, of which they have no fear. For this reason they must always be kept leashed in public. At home, they definitely need a fenced yard.

Special Perks: Cavaliers are devoted to children and good with other pets, be they feline or canine. This breed's coat needs regular brushing, but not trimming.

Bugs in the System: Hereditary problems include early onset of a dangerous heart condition called mitral valve disease, slipped kneecaps, hip dysplasia, and a neurological condition known as syringomyelia. The floppy ears need regular cleaning.

If someone broke into my house, this dog would: Be deadly in close-quarters combat. Just kidding! It's worthless as a watchdog. The only way it could harm a burglar is if the guy tripped over it.

If you like the cavalier, check out: The near-ubiquitous cocker spaniel. Or, if all you really want is a perky, sociable lapdog, the bichon frise.

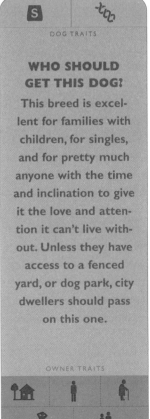

DOG TRAITS

WHO SHOULD GET THIS DOG?
This breed is excellent for families with children, for singles, and for pretty much anyone with the time and inclination to give it the love and attention it can't live without. Unless they have access to a fenced yard, or dog park, city dwellers should pass on this one.

OWNER TRAITS

Weight: *55–80 pounds (24.8–36.0 kg).* **Height:** *21–26 inches (53.3–66.0 cm).* **Build:** *Muscular and athletic.* **Coat:** *Rough, thick, and oily coat, usually in solid dark colors such as brown and tan.* **Brains:** *Very smart (it is well known for being able to remember the locations of several ducks at once) but sometimes difficult to train.* **Bladder Matters:** *No special house-training issues.*

The Incredible Origin: This breed was allegedly created when two Newfoundlands that survived the wreck of a British ship off the Maryland coast were mated to local retrievers. The result is not the most attractive dog in the world, but certainly one of the best hunting companions. Its thick, waterproof coat makes it invulnerable to cold and wet, and its webbed toes help make it a strong swimmer.

Trademark Traits: Friendly and loving to its family and also to properly introduced strangers, the Chesapeake is nevertheless a tougher customer than your typical Labrador or golden retriever. First and foremost, it can be combative with other dogs.

Headaches and Hassles: Maybe it's the Newfoundland in them, but Chesapeakes are peculiarly strong—which makes careful training even more important.

Special Perks: The Chesapeake is an excellent jogging or biking companion. It is also a guardian of children and over the decades has saved more than a few from drowning.

Bugs in the System: Generally healthy, though some suffer from eye problems and hip dysplasia.

If someone broke into my house, this dog would: Alert you early and loudly. The Chesapeake is very protective of its family and can be quite territorial, which is something of an oddity in a retriever.

If you like the Chesapeake Bay retriever, check out: The much-easier-to-obtain golden retriever and Labrador retriever.

DOG TRAITS

WHO SHOULD GET THIS DOG?

This is a no-nonsense hunting breed. Unless you spend a good portion of each fall sitting in a duck blind (or live in the woods, beside a lake), leave the Chesapeake Bay retriever to the professionals. Both you and the dog will be happier.

OWNER TRAITS

Chihuahua

Weight: *2–6 pounds (0.9–2.7 kg).* **Height:** *6–9 inches (15.2–22.9 cm).* **Build:** *As fragile as a baby bird.* **Coat:** *Available in short-haired and long-haired varieties, and in a wide range of colors and color combinations.* **Brains:** *Capable of learning a full retinue of tricks.* **Bladder Matters:** *No special house-training problems.*

The Incredible Origin: This breed's boosters like to say it's been knocking around Mexico since pre-Columbian days, while others maintain it's a European variety that came over with the conquistadores. The truth is, no one really knows. What *is* known is that late nineteenth-century American tourists started buying them and hauling them back to the States, where the tiny dog became a huge hit. Selective breeding gave it a distinctive domed head and bulging, big eyes worthy of those velvet paintings of pixies and street urchins. In the early days, the first, fragile, short-haired specimens were "toughened up" by crossings with terriers. The long-haired variety was allegedly created by pairing it with papillons (see page 146), Pomeranians (see page 149) and, perhaps, other small breeds.

Trademark Traits: The Chihuahua is the world's smallest dog. However, it doesn't seem to realize this. The little canine is so full of fire that it will sometimes challenge dogs twenty times its size. It can love its owner to the point of possessiveness and will relentlessly seek attention. However, it's so precious and loving, it's able to get along with other dogs and cats, and it is very much at home in almost any accommodation, be it a mansion or studio apartment. It is still the compact companion of choice for society divas, including Paris Hilton and Madonna (whose pint-size posse member is named Chiquita).

Headaches and Hassles: Long-haired Chihuahuas need regular combing. The short-haired version can suffer from the cold, so stock up on cute, dinky sweaters. Seriously. Look on the Internet, and you'll discover an entire Chihuahua sweater *industry.* Also: Small children can frighten Chihuahuas, and for good reason. This extremely fragile dog can easily be injured by rough or clumsy handling. If cornered by an inquisitive toddler, this canine will almost certainly bite.

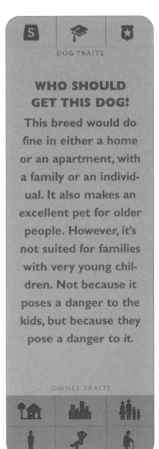

DOG TRAITS

WHO SHOULD GET THIS DOG?

This breed would do fine in either a home or an apartment, with a family or an individual. It also makes an excellent pet for older people. However, it's not suited for families with very young children. Not because it poses a danger to the kids, but because they pose a danger to *it.*

OWNER TRAITS

Special Perks: The Chihuahua is a highly entertaining dog in an extremely petite package—easy to feed, easy to exercise, easy to care for. A romp around the living room, a little kibble, and your presence are pretty much all it needs.

Bugs in the System: Chihuahuas have an absolutely appalling sense of smell. They also have a space in the tops of their skulls that can make them vulnerable to head injury. Beware of extremely puny specimens sometimes called "teacup" Chihuahuas. They are not a separate breed, but rather undersized versions of *this* breed—often too delicate and tiny to be viable.

If someone broke into my house, this dog would: Bark as loud as its teeny, squeaky voice would allow.

If you like Chihuahuas, check out: The sweet-tempered papillon, which looks a lot like a Chihuahua because the two types were interbred. Or try another possible member of this breed's family tree, the almost-as-tiny Pomeranian.

Weight: Up to 12 pounds (5.4 kg). Height: 9–13 inches (22.9–33 cm). Build: Very graceful and fragile. Coat: One type of Chinese crested, known as the powder puff, has a long, gossamer coat over a wooly undercoat. The other type is hairless except for its feet, the end of its tail, and the top of its head. Brains: Average intelligence; amenable to training. Bladder Matters: No special house-training issues.

The Incredible Origin: The crested is allegedly of Chinese ancestry, though evidence supporting this is very thin. It is similar to the Mexican hairless (see page 140).

Trademark Traits: The crested, both hairy and hairless, needs to be with its owner all the time. *All* the time. If you are standing, it will be at your feet. If you are sitting, it will be on your lap. And it's going to sleep with you, so get used to the idea. If it feels it's not getting enough attention, a crested may bark excessively, show aggression, backslide on its house-training, or develop obsessive tics such as spinning.

Headaches and Hassles: The hairy version, called the powder puff, needs daily brushing to keep its long coat in order. The hairless version requires regular baths, lotion for its skin, sunscreen in summer, and sweaters in winter.

Special Perks: For obvious reasons, the hairless version neither sheds nor harbors fleas. Its exercise needs are very modest, and its personality is particularly endearing. Cresteds love to romp, and if the spirit moves them, they will "sing" in a high, lilting howl.

Bugs in the System: This breed has two obvious problems (a vulnerability to sunburn and excessive cold) and one not-so-obvious foible—it's allergic to wool. So keep this in mind while shopping for tiny, tiny coats. The teeth of the hairless crested are often thin and misaligned, with some actually missing.

If someone broke into my house, this dog would: Bark. Hopefully. It's not much of a watchdog.

If you like the Chinese crested, check out: The equally naked Mexican hairless.

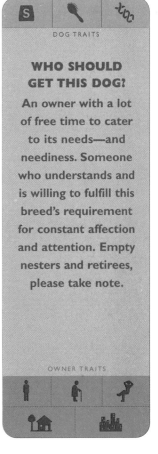

DOG TRAITS

WHO SHOULD GET THIS DOG?

An owner with a lot of free time to cater to its needs—and neediness. Someone who understands and is willing to fulfill this breed's requirement for constant affection and attention. Empty nesters and retirees, please take note.

OWNER TRAITS

*Weight: 40–55 pounds (18–24.8 kg). **Height:** 18–25 inches (45.7–63.5 cm). **Build:** Solid and muscular. **Coat:** Short, rough coat in colors ranging from black to fawn to cream. **Brains:** Intelligent, but can be stubborn when it comes to training. **Bladder Matters:** No particular house-training problems.*

The Incredible Origin: This bizarre-looking canine was used for centuries in China as a hunting and fighting dog (the loose skin allowed it to dodge fatal bites). It was almost wiped out after the Communists took control, but it survived through the efforts of breeders in Hong Kong and America. The shar-pei comes in two varieties: super-wrinkled and only mildly wrinkled. Like Chow Chows, shar-peis have bluish-black tongues.

Trademark Traits: The shar-pei will clown around with its family, but around strangers it can act aloof, though rarely overly suspicious. The word "arrogant" is often used to describe its attitude.

Headaches and Hassles: Shar-peis must be carefully trained. Because they can be combative with unfamiliar dogs, they must always be leashed in public. Plus, this dog may constantly rub its rough coat against you—to the point where some owners actually develop a mild form of contact dermititis.

Special Perks: A well-trained, well-socialized shar-pei can make an excellent addition to your family.

Bugs in the System: The shar-pei is heir to a number of genetic problems, including a raft of eye issues. Because their eyes are so deep set, they have very poor peripheral vision. The dogs are also vulnerable to ear infections and various skin irritations, from dermatitis to demodectic mange. That wrinkly skin provides lots of hiding places for mites, moisture, and other sources of dermatological mayhem.

If someone broke into my house, this dog would: Serve up a steaming plate of stir-fried whoopass with noodles on the side.

If you like the shar-pei, check out: The not-quite-as-wrinkly English bulldog.

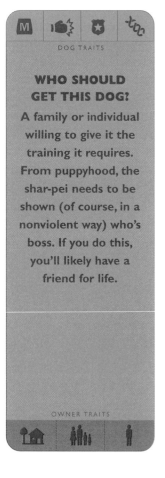

DOG TRAITS

WHO SHOULD GET THIS DOG?

A family or individual willing to give it the training it requires. From puppyhood, the shar-pei needs to be shown (of course, in a nonviolent way) who's boss. If you do this, you'll likely have a friend for life.

OWNER TRAITS

Weight: 45–80 pounds (20.3–36 kg). **Height:** 16–21 inches (40.6–53.3 cm). **Build:** Stocky and powerful. **Coat:** Very thick double coat in various solid colors ranging from black to red. **Brains:** A chow can be trained, but it can be very disinterested and willful. You must be strong and assertive when handling this dog, but never resort to corporal punishment—unless you want to wind up on the next installment of When Animals Attack. **Bladder Matters:** No special house-training problems.

The Incredible Origin: A descendant of dogs used for hundreds of years in China as hunters and guardians, the chow chow was brought to the West at the beginning of the nineteenth century. Home decorating expert and convicted felon Martha Stewart owns this breed.

Trademark Traits: The chow was originally a hunting and guarding dog, and it still acts the part. Remember James Bond's nemesis Oddjob from *Goldfinger*? They could have modeled his character after this breed. Reserved even with its family, it can be downright paranoid around unfamiliar faces. This dog is strong willed, and it must be socialized and trained from an early age if it is to become a safe, well-mannered pet. *If you aren't willing to invest lots of time in training, do not get a chow.* Also: Don't get this dog if you're trying to make some kind of macho statement. The only statement you'll make is, "I am a person with very poor judgment who shouldn't be trusted with a sharp stick, let alone a big, potentially dangerous dog."

Headaches and Hassles: Even with regular grooming, every piece of clothing you own will be accented with chow hair. This goes double for spring and fall, when this breed sheds its massive undercoat. The chow is aggressive toward other dogs, particularly those of the same sex. Some have no problem with cats. They see them, they kill them. No problem. For this reason (and a bunch of others) chows must always be leashed in public. Finally, acquire your dog from a high-quality breeder. This is not the sort of canine you want to get from a pet store or from a neighbor down the street who's giving puppies away.

DOG TRAITS

WHO SHOULD GET THIS DOG?

Chow chows are for experienced dog owners. This naturally aggressive canine requires a tremendous amount of training and socialization—more than the average person is typically willing to give. It's not a good choice for families with babies and toddlers—or for couples who plan to start a family.

OWNER TRAITS

Special Perks: This dog possesses head-turning looks, makes a very effective guard dog, and rarely barks excessively. A regular walk satisfies its exercise needs. Plus, a carefully raised chow can be very loyal and loving to its master.

Bugs in the System: Prone to hip dysplasia, hypothyroidism, entropion (inverted eyelids), and other genetic disorders. Heavy-coated chow chows also have a lot of trouble in hot weather. During warmer seasons, keep it in the air-conditioning and curtail outdoor activities.

If someone broke into my house, this dog would: Rip him to shreds. The typical chow can be problematic enough with *benign* strangers. Anyone with truly malicious intent will probably wind up looking like they lost a fight with a wood chipper.

If you like the chow chow, check out: The less-twitchy but still exotic-looking Chinese shar-pei.

Weight: *20–35 pounds (9–15.8 kg).* **Height:** *12–16 inches (30.5–40.6 cm).* **Build:** *Sturdy and solid.* **Coat:** *Long, flowing hair in colors ranging from solid black to solid gold to mixes.* **Brains:** *Usually quite intelligent. However, training can be an involved process.* **Bladder Matters:** *Can be tricky to house-train.*

The Incredible Origin: The poor "cocker" is living proof that it's possible to be too popular. Originally bred as a hunting dog in England (it was called a cocker because it hunted, among other things, woodcocks), it was imported to America, down-sized, and became for many years the most popular breed in the United States. It has diverged so markedly from the British version that it is now considered a separate line. Indiscriminate reproduction to meet demand did great damage to this dog, loading it with genetic and mental defects that still bedevil it today.

Trademark Traits: The typical, healthy cocker is happy, exuberant, and an ideal companion for children who are old enough to respect it. It loves its master and can get very, very excited when he or she comes home from work. It can also be (and in some cases, still is) trained as a gun dog. It can flush game and then, on command, retrieve the kill. Not that there's much call for this out in suburbia, which is where you'll find most of today's cockers.

Headaches and Hassles: The cocker's luxurious hair must be combed more or less daily, washed frequently, and professionally groomed regularly. This hassle can be lessened by giving the dog a shorter utility cut, but you're still going to know a groomer on a first-name basis. To avoid infection, the dog's long, floppy ears must be cleaned religiously.

Special Perks: A cocker will adapt to pretty much any situation in which it finds itself. If you like to take it on long walks, it will be first out the door. If you like to pile up on the couch, it will snuggle right up beside you (though it's still advisable to give it regular exercise). As for living arrangements, an apartment or a mansion is fine, as long as you're there with it.

DOG TRAITS

WHO SHOULD GET THIS DOG?

A family or individual willing to give it the affection and training it needs—and who is prepared, financially and emotionally, to cope with any medical problems that may surface. Someone like, say, Oscar-winning actress Charlize Theron, who has two.

OWNER TRAITS

Bugs in the System: The roster of issues includes, but is by no means confined to, spinal problems, various eye disorders, skin problems, and a truly frightening neurological disease called rage syndrome. It's something like epilepsy, except that afflicted dogs don't have seizures. Instead, they fly into a blind, uncontrolled rage. *Because the cocker has been so severely overbred, obtaining one from a careful, qualified breeder is extremely important.*

If someone broke into my house, this dog would: Bark incessantly. In spite of its size, the typical cocker spaniel makes a very good security guard.

If you like the cocker, check out: The elegant and somewhat harder to obtain cavalier King Charles spaniel, or the somewhat larger, but just as loving and devoted, Brittany.

Weight: 48–70 pounds (21.6–31.5 kg). **Height:** 22–24 inches (55.9–61 cm). **Build:** Graceful. **Coat:** Long, flowing hair in sable and white, tricolor, and blue merle. **Brains:** Highly intelligent, if somewhat twitchy. **Bladder Matters:** No special house-training issues.

The Incredible Origin: A former herding dog from the Scottish lowlands, this canine got its name from the colley sheep it often tended. Not surprisingly, the original version bore only a passing resemblance to the refined creature we see today—an animal created through decades of selective breeding in Great Britain and the United States. Legend has it that the dog's thick mane was developed so it could stand for hours in the face of gale-force winds. One of the breed's first celebrity boosters was reportedly Queen Victoria, who in the 1860s brought several back to England from Scotland, triggering the beginning of the collie craze—a craze that, in some circles, has never really ended.

Trademark Traits: One could get the impression, based on the breed's press clippings, that collies are highly intelligent, easygoing animals who get along with almost anyone. This isn't exactly true. Collies are smart, but they can also be wary around people they don't know (unfortunately, some collies may classify your next-door neighbor, who's been over hundreds of times, as "people they don't know"). Their quirky personalities, an odd mix of brittle emotionalism with a spritz of passive-aggressiveness, also make them tricky to train. If you get angry at a collie it may pout and sulk in a very dramatic, Elizabeth-Taylor-refusing-to-come-out-of-her-trailer sort of way. So just as with Ms. Taylor, the collie must be lavished with lots of positive reinforcement if you want to get a good performance out of it. Here's something else to consider: While the collie can be an excellent pet, and quite beautiful, *it is not Lassie*. It cannot perform long division. It cannot understand complex conversations. And if Timmy falls down the well, it probably won't run to the farmhouse for help. So dial back those expectations.

Headaches and Hassles: Drag a comb through this dog's mane

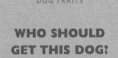

DOG TRAITS

WHO SHOULD GET THIS DOG?
A family with kids that can provide the emotional attention this dog craves. Remember that while a collie isn't everybody's best friend, it will be utterly devoted to you and yours. Be advised that while adult collies can be calm and steady, the puppies are quite rambunctious.

OWNER TRAITS

daily and have it professionally groomed regularly. Otherwise it will look like Jessica Simpson's head exploded in your living room. If you don't want to make like Vidal Sassoon every day, you can get a short-haired version called a "smooth" collie. Physically and mentally it's just like the long-haired or "rough" variety. It just isn't as glamorous.

Special Perks: Though the collie's coat is high maintenance, almost nothing else about it is. The dog doesn't dig destructively and doesn't require heroic physical activity. Regular walks are appreciated, as are occasional trips to the dog park for off-lead runs (though some collies—this is no exaggeration—seem to resent mixing with the hoi polloi in such settings). Remember that the collie's heavy coat makes summer fun problematic. In August yours may prefer to spend the daylight hours sleeping on top of an air-conditioning vent.

Bugs in the System: Collies can suffer from vision problems and hip dysplasia.

If someone broke into my house, this dog would: Bark to raise the alarm, and then, if the situation deteriorated, probably wade in. Back in the day, these animals didn't just herd sheep. They also repelled wolf attacks. If its family is threatened, the typical collie can still throw down.

If you like collies, check out: The Shetland sheepdog (sheltie), which looks like (and, for all intents and purposes, is) a miniaturized collie.

Dachshund

Weight: 16–32 pounds (standard) (7.2–14.4 kg); up to 11 pounds (miniature) (5 kg). **Height:** 8 inches (standard) (20.3 cm); 6 inches (miniature) (15.2 cm). **Build:** Long and low. **Coat:** Available in short, long, and wiry coats, and in a variety of colors and color combinations. **Brains:** Intelligent but willful, à la the terrier. Training must be consistent, positive, and ongoing. **Bladder Matters:** No particular house-training issues.

The Incredible Origin: People who like the dachshund simply for its looks may have trouble wrapping their minds around the idea that it isn't a lapdog. This funny-looking breed was developed in Germany to chase, fight, and kill everything from foxes to badgers. Famous for its tenacity, it could allegedly track a wounded animal for days once it got a scent of its blood. Try *that* with a Chihuahua or a pug. The dachshund is available in two sizes, standard and miniature.

Trademark Traits: To reiterate, *this is no lapdog*. When it comes to energy, exuberance, and sheer bloody-mindedness, the dachshund (translation: "badger dog") works hard and plays hard. Get on its good side, and you've earned the friendship of an interesting, lovable companion. Just don't expect it to sit on the couch all day. As a matter of fact it probably shouldn't be on the couch *at all*, given its twitchy back (see below).

Headaches and Hassles: A dachshund needs regular walks and off-lead playtime. Be advised that if it doesn't burn off its energy this way, it will do it some other way. A way that may involve property damage. For a number of reasons (including its relative fragility) it isn't good in homes with very small children. Dachshunds can be relentless diggers, combative with other dogs, and easily distracted by unfamiliar smells. They will also pursue and attack small game, be it a squirrel at the park or a gerbil in your daughter's bedroom. This breed should always be leashed in public. Dachshunds also overeat and can become fat.

Special Perks: A well-trained, happy dachshund makes an incredibly entertaining companion. This breed can be quite long-lived, and its hair is easy to groom.

DOG TRAITS

WHO SHOULD GET THIS DOG?

A single person or a family with older children who can give it careful attention and training. The dachshund can get along well in an apartment, provided it gets regular walks (and provided it doesn't go into barking fits when you aren't home).

OWNER TRAITS

Bugs in the System: The wiener dog's back is a source of unending trouble. Because it can easily herniate a disk, causing incredible pain or even paralysis of the rear legs, the dog should be discouraged from jumping off of things such as beds and couches. Also, watch its weight, because excess poundage can wreak havoc. The breed also faces various eye and skin disorders, cardiac disease, and diabetes. For these reasons and others, it is important to acquire a dachshund from a responsible breeder or other reputable source.

If someone broke into my house, this dog would: Greet him with furious barking and, perhaps, even a frontal assault. Even under the *best* of circumstances, Dachshunds can be pissy with strangers.

If you like the dachshund, check out: The equally scrappy (but comparatively more sturdy) Border terrier. Or if you're really into low-slung dogs with attitude, the Dandie Dinmont terrier.

Weight: *45–70 pounds (20.3–31.5 kg).* **Height:** *19–24 inches (48.3–61 cm).* **Build:** *Sleek and muscular.* **Coat:** *Extremely short hair, white with black or liver spots. Puppies are born solid white.* **Brains:** *Intelligent, but sometimes can be difficult to train, especially if negative reinforcement is used. Positive reinforcement gets markedly better results.* **Bladder Matters:** *No particular house-training problems.*

The Incredible Origin: No one can say for sure how the word "Dalmatian" became associated with this breed, which claims no particularly strong connection to the region of Dalmatia. All that's known is that in nineteenth-century Europe they became premier "coach dogs," riding along (or, more often, running beside) everything from hacks to, most famously, horse-drawn fire trucks. During runs they helped calm the horses and guard the equipment. The movie *101 Dalmatians* turned a dog that's definitely not for everyone into a popular sensation. Not only did legions of people who had no business having one acquire them (and then, shortly thereafter, abandon them), it also encouraged indiscriminate breeding to fill the demand.

Trademark Traits: A well-bred, well-trained Dalmatian is intelligent, energetic, devoted to its family, and a particular friend of older, respectful children. It also makes an excellent running/biking partner. When happy, the Dalmatian will curl its lips into a teeth-baring smile. This can be quite endearing if you know what it's doing and quite unsettling if you don't.

Headaches and Hassles: The important thing to remember is that the Dalmatian was once used to guard carriages. *Guard* them. Some can display territorial and aggressive tendencies not too dissimilar from those of, say, a Doberman pinscher or German shepherd. They are very exuberant and can bowl over small children or the elderly. Also, Dalmatians shed constantly, and their hair clings with great tenacity to upholstery and clothing. Dalmatians suffer from the cold and shouldn't stay outside for more than 15 minutes without some sort of protection (yes, a sweater). The Dalmatian likes to wander and should always be leashed in public. Finally, remember that this breed expects to be

DOG TRAITS

WHO SHOULD GET THIS DOG?
This dog can be excellent for families with older children, provided it is well trained, carefully socialized, and comes from good genetic stock. You should be prepared, however, to provide daily exercise. Dalmatians need to stay on an even keel—just like Richard Simmons, who owns half a dozen of them.

OWNER TRAITS

a member of your family. If it feels that it isn't, you could be in for a load of black-and-white spotted trouble. Neglected or poorly socialized dogs can register their displeasure with excessive digging, excessive barking, excessive territoriality, even excessive aggressiveness.

Special Perks: A well-trained, well-socialized Dalmatian makes an excellent companion for both adults and older children. To underscore a point made earlier, this dog's potential as an exercise/jogging partner should not be underestimated. If it could keep up with a careening horse-drawn fire truck, it can no doubt keep up with you.

Bugs in the System: Around 10 percent of Dalmatians are born deaf. Approximately 20 percent can only hear in one ear. This breed is subject to skin allergies and needs a special diet to prevent bladder stones. These dogs are also prone to a poorly understood, rather gross condition called "Dal crud." It causes the skin to break out in small, itchy, seeping lesions that can permanently discolor the coat.

If someone broke into my house, this dog would: Wake the dead with its furious barking, then open up a can of four-alarm whoopass.

If you like the Dalmatian, check out: The Labrador retriever, which offers roughly the same size body, but with less attitude.

Weight: 18–24 pounds (8.1–10.8 kg). *Height:* 8–11 inches (20.3–27.9 cm). *Build:* Short legs, dachshundlike body. *Coat:* Long, rough outer coat, in traditional colors of "pepper" (bluish-black to pale gray) and "mustard" (various shades of reddish-brown). *Brains:* Dandies are very intelligent and capable of mastering complex training—if they feel like it. To make sure they feel like it, always teach them in a positive, upbeat way. *Bladder Matters:* No special house-training problems.

The Incredible Origin: Developed on the English/Scottish border, this odd-looking breed got its odd-sounding name from a character in the 1815 Sir Walter Scott novel *Guy Mannering*. But though they look fancy, "Dandies" were bred to hunt and kill vermin.

Trademark Traits: Dandies are tough little dogs who are devoted to their families. They are good with older children (8 years old and up), and can be good with cats and other dogs. However, they can't be trusted around preylike animals such as hamsters and rats. These canines have a lot of moxie and may try to dominate a weak owner.

Headaches and Hassles: Maintaining the Dandie's look of studied unkemptness requires lots of home combing, plus regular visits to the groomer. Dandies like to dig, and they will tunnel under a backyard fence if given half a chance. Careful training, regular exercise, and close supervision can mitigate this problem. Dandies will compulsively chase anything that flees, so they must always be kept leashed in public. Also, these dogs tend to overeat.

Special Perks: A well-trained Dandie offers the spunk and personality of a terrier, but in a cuter, somewhat less hyper package.

Bugs in the System: These dogs, for obvious reasons, can have back problems. It is important to always set a Dandie down on all four feet at once—never on just the front feet or back feet, because this can aggravate any nascent spine issues.

If someone broke into my house, this dog would: Probably announce any intruder with a tremendous blast of barking.

If you like the Dandie Dinmont, check out: The similarly elongated dachshund.

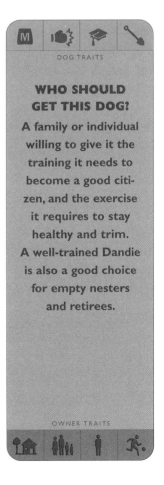

DOG TRAITS

WHO SHOULD GET THIS DOG?

A family or individual willing to give it the training it needs to become a good citizen, and the exercise it requires to stay healthy and trim. A well-trained Dandie is also a good choice for empty nesters and retirees.

OWNER TRAITS

Weight: 66–88 pounds (29.7–39.6 kg). *Height:* 24–28 inches (61–71.1 cm). *Build:* Streamlined but well-muscled. *Coat:* Extremely short hair. Black with tan markings is the most common color scheme, but red, fawn, blue, and brown are also available. *Brains:* Dobermans are extremely intelligent, eager to learn, and capable of handling the most complex training. *Bladder Matters:* No special house-training problems.

The Incredible Origin: While many famous guarding breeds were originally developed to do other things (German shepherds herded sheep and Rottweilers herded cattle), from Day One the Doberman was designed to do only *one* thing—put the hurt to the bad guys. It was developed by Louis Dobermann, a nineteenth-century German tax collector who wanted first-class protection on his daily rounds. Using stock from the local animal shelter (where he worked as a keeper), he gradually developed his ultimate dream—and the ultimate nightmare for muggers and second-story men the world over. Today's "Dobie" (which apparently is much less ferocious than Herr Dobermann's original version) is a favorite for military work and guard duty, and it makes an excellent service dog as well. By the way, "pinscher" means "biter" in German.

Trademark Traits: At one time the Dobie was Lucifer's lapdog. It was so ferocious that one great champion allegedly won dog shows even though some of its teeth were missing—a fact the judges overlooked, because none had the guts to pry its mouth open. Today's carefully bred canines are far less wantonly aggressive. Still, they remain extremely protective of their homes and families, and they are deeply suspicious of strangers. They harbor strong aggressive tendencies and display dominant personalities that can lead some to challenge their owners.

Headaches and Hassles: Because it is naturally aggressive and dominant, a Dobie must be carefully trained and socialized from puppyhood. If you don't have the time or inclination to do this, do yourself and the dog a favor and choose a less-challenging breed. Also, this dog has absolutely no business in a family with very small children.

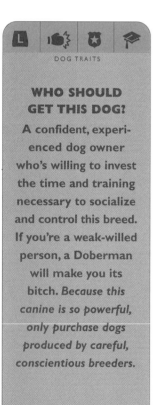

DOG TRAITS

WHO SHOULD GET THIS DOG?

A confident, experienced dog owner who's willing to invest the time and training necessary to socialize and control this breed. If you're a weak-willed person, a Doberman will make you its bitch. *Because this canine is so powerful, only purchase dogs produced by careful, conscientious breeders.*

OWNER TRAITS

Special Perks: In spite of this canine's fearsome (and richly deserved) reputation, a well-bred, well-trained Doberman can be a devoted friend—a friend who's indifferent to physical pain and just might save your life someday.

Bugs in the System: A Doberman's ears must be surgically altered to obtain their intimidating points. Left as God intended them, they are disarmingly floppy. This breed can also suffer from a long list of genetic defects, including heart disease, various eye disorders, bloat, and hip dysplasia. Because of their short, sleek coats, Dobies don't do well in extreme cold.

If someone broke into my house, this dog would: Hurt someone. Badly. And that someone will not be you.

If you like the Doberman, check out: The Rottweiler, which looks somewhat like a Doberman that's spent a lot of time working with free weights. Or the Dalmatian, which, in spite of what you may have seen in *101 Dalmatians*, is a very effective guardian.

Dogo Argentino

Weight: 80–100 pounds (36–45 kg). *Height:* 24–27 inches (60–69 cm). *Build:* Compact and extremely muscular. *Coat:* Short, thick, smooth, and white fur. *Brains:* In Argentina the Dogo has been everything from a police dog to a guide dog for the visually impaired. It can handle a lot of training, but instruction must be offered patiently and without corporal punishment. *Bladder Matters:* No particular house-training problems.

The Incredible Origin: This breed was created by two Argentine brothers who spent decades building the perfect boar-hunting dog. They did this by mixing nine different breeds (including the boxer, Great Dane, bulldog, bull terrier, Spanish mastiff, Irish wolfhound, Great Pyrenees, and a local pit fighter called the Cordoba dog) to create what looks like a huge, snow-white American Staffordshire terrier.

Trademark Traits: The Dogo is devoted to its family and tolerant of (human) guests. However, one should never forget that this dog was bred for battle. It needs careful training.

Headaches and Hassles: This is a very, very powerful dog, and one that is inappropriate for a physically or psychologically weak person. Because the Dogo contains so much potential for mayhem (it doesn't particularly like other dogs and can suffer from separation anxiety if left alone too long), it must be well trained and ready to respond to your commands. Because it can be distracted by interesting sights, it cannot be trusted off its lead in public.

Special Perks: The Dogo's short coat is relatively easy to care for. Also, it is arguably more "steady" than its mirror image, the American Staffordshire terrier.

Bugs in the System: The dog, perhaps owing to its cosmopolitan makeup, is mostly free of genetic foibles. However, it does have one, and it's a biggie—about 10 percent of Dogos are born deaf. Also, the breed is prone to sunburn.

If someone broke into my house, this dog would: Not hesitate to defend its family. Like most big, truly scary dogs, the Dogo usually doesn't go nuts barking at people. Its actions speak louder than words.

If you like the Dogo Argentino, check out: The Dogo's physical (though not mental) clone, the American Staffordshire terrier.

DOG TRAITS

WHO SHOULD GET THIS DOG?

Unless you've got a wild boar problem in your neighborhood, the Dogo is probably too much canine for you. However, if you do get one, make sure you've got the psychological strength to keep it under control and the willingness to invest considerable time in training.

OWNER TRAITS

*Weight: 99–150 pounds (45–68 kg). **Height:** 23–27 inches (58.4–68.6 cm). **Build:** Massive head on an equally massive body. **Coat:** Very short, usually fawn-colored hair. **Brains:** Can be somewhat resistant to training. Should be socialized from an early age to children, other dogs, and people in general. **Bladder Matters:** No particular house-training problems.*

The Incredible Origin: The true story of this breed is probably irretrievably lost. However, its "other name," the French mastiff, gives a pretty strong clue as to who contributed most strongly to its current appearance—and to its former work as a guardian and war dog. By the way, if this breed looks familiar, you're probably remembering the canine star of the 1989 movie *Turner & Hooch.*

Trademark Traits: While this isn't the scariest dog on the planet, its wrinkly, scowling face makes it arguably the scariest *looking*. Still, if need be, this naturally territorial, highly protective breed is ready, willing, and able to back up its intimidating visage. The Dogue de Bordeaux is very "dominant" and can push around a weak owner.

Headaches and Hassles: The Dogue sheds constantly, and its drool output has to be seen to be believed. This dog also isn't a good choice for the elderly or for homes with small children. When the Dogue gets rambunctious, which it does from time to time, it can easily lay out an NFL linebacker. It can also be aggressive toward other dogs.

Special Perks: In general, the Dogue is placid and even-tempered with its family. Its chief concerns are (1) being near you, and (2) finding a comfortable place to sleep.

Bugs in the System: Common maladies include hip dysplasia, heart problems, skin diseases, and bloat.

If someone broke into my house, this dog would: React in a very violent, very definitive, and very *un*-French way.

If you like the Dogue de Bordeaux, check out: The bullmastiff and mastiff, which offer the same body type—and, sad to say, similar volumes of drool.

DOG TRAITS

WHO SHOULD GET THIS DOG?

A strong-willed individual or a family (without very young children) who can provide the care, discipline, and training this breed requires. Though big, the Dogue isn't particularly athletic. So if you're looking for a jogging partner, keep looking.

OWNER TRAITS

Fox Terrier

*Weight: 13–20 pounds (5.9–9 kg). **Height:** 13–16 inches (33–40.6 cm). **Build:** Muscular but slender. **Coat:** Available in smooth or wiry coats. Both varieties are white with dark markings. **Brains:** Extremely intelligent, though difficult to train. The only method that works is positive reinforcement. Start yelling at or otherwise abusing your fox terrier and you've lost the battle. **Bladder Matters:** No special house-training issues.*

The Incredible Origin: The fox terrier was developed in the nineteenth century to assist in (big surprise) fox hunting. After the hounds had chased the fox into its den, this little dog was often employed to chase it right back out (they also make excellent ratters). Other than their hairstyles, the smooth and wiry-coated types are identical. Another interesting feature is that these small dogs seem to possess Doberman-sized teeth.

Trademark Traits: Like most other terriers, this variety is combative, intelligent, and wrapped as tight as an overwound watch. This incredibly strong-willed breed loves to run and play and wants to be with its family 24 hours a day. Be warned that if it feels neglected, behavioral problems—the kinds of behavioral problems that may force you to buy a new couch—will quickly surface. This breed is a superstar athlete, capable of leaping a standard-issue chain-link fence in a single bound.

Headaches and Hassles: This high-energy dog must be carefully trained and socialized from puppyhood, if you want it to be a well-mannered, placid adult. The fox terrier can be incurably, almost jubilantly, aggressive toward other dogs. It might lay into your neighbor's German shepherd with the same gusto that some breeds reserve for games of fetch. For this reason it can't be trusted off its leash in public. It also can't be left unsupervised in your backyard, because it can leap over or tunnel under pretty much any barrier. Fox terriers like to bark, and if they feel neglected they can make it a habit—an unbelievably annoying habit. They also can't be trusted around small animals such as rats and gerbils. And if you want them to get along with cats, you'd better intro-

DOG TRAITS

WHO SHOULD GET THIS DOG?

A family or individual willing to provide the training—and the long walks—this exuberant dog needs to thrive. A large, well-secured backyard is a big plus. Older, well-trained fox terriers can adjust to apartment life.

OWNER TRAITS

duce them to some at a very early age. They are problematic around very young children, who might be frightened by this breed's in-your-face attitude. Now before you hurry to the next page, keep reading to discover the *good* habits of this breed.

Special Perks: The fox terrier is one of those rare breeds that can display near-*Lassie*-like courage and resourcefulness when aiding its family—saving children from burning houses, fending off wild animals, that sort of thing. If you can get on the good side of one of these little guys, you've made a true friend—the kind who'll always have your back in a crisis.

Bugs in the System: Though in general a healthy breed, the fox terrier can suffer from eye problems and skin allergies.

If someone broke into my house, this dog would: Raise the devil himself with its barking, and then, in all likelihood, attack. An aroused fox terrier knows no fear.

If you like the fox terrier, check out: The slightly smaller but just-as-tough Jack Russell terrier, and the larger but just-as-tough Airedale.

Weight: 60–85 pounds (27–38.3 kg). **Height:** *23–25 inches (58.4–63.5 cm).* **Build:** *Powerful, well-muscled, wolflike body.* **Coat:** *Dense, medium-length hair, primarily brown with black markings.* **Brains:** *This is one of the easiest of all breeds to train—primarily because the German shepherd was designed as a working dog and seems to relish being put through its paces.* **Bladder Matters:** *No special house-training problems.*

The Incredible Origin: This massive, deeply intimidating Teutonic warrior was originally used to herd *sheep.* So just how big are German sheep, anyway? Developed in the nineteenth century from several varieties of homegrown sheepdog, its intelligence and trainability have earned it the canine world's most varied portfolio of jobs—everything from guide dog to war dog to police dog.

Trademark Traits: Two traits define the German shepherd—high intelligence and high energy. This dog was bred to work, so it won't tolerate lazing on the couch all day, waiting for you to come home, and then lazing on the couch all evening, waiting for you to go to bed. The shepherd requires interesting activities, careful training, and, most importantly, a strong hand. It will not automatically accept you as its master. You will have to earn that title—and probably keep earning it for the rest of the dog's life.

Headaches and Hassles: Shepherds shed like crazy, especially during fall and spring, when they "blow" their coats. So you might want to lay up a big supply of vacuum cleaner bags come April and October. Also, if bored, they can become quite destructive, digging up the yard, trashing home furnishings, and making a general nuisance of themselves. Some, just to find something to do, will "herd" the family children. The shepherd must always be engaged and stimulated, and carefully trained to make sure its aggressive tendencies remain in check. This task never ends.

Special Perks: If you give a shepherd what it needs, it will become everything you could possibly want, including a friend of children, a fearless, disciplined guardian, and a devoted companion.

DOG TRAITS

WHO SHOULD GET THIS DOG?

An energetic individual or family that understands the necessary commitment to create a disciplined, loving shepherd. Since these dogs respect firm leadership, it's also a good idea to make sure you're not living with a milquetoast who can't control the dog when you're not around.

OWNER TRAITS

Bugs in the System: Shepherds, particularly poorly bred ones, tend to suffer from hip dysplasia. Other problems include eczema and inflammation of the cornea. Many retain puppylike attitudes and energy levels into their second and third years. Poorly bred dogs can also suffer from mental tics ranging from excessive shyness to viciousness. By the way, please don't get a shepherd because you think it will make you look macho. People who are *that* concerned about their machismo probably aren't macho enough to handle one.

If someone broke into my house, this dog would: Warn him off with savage barking. But if the poor schlep proceeded to break in anyway, the shepherd would bite him. Repeatedly. They're very, very good at biting things and, when circumstances warrant, they really seem to enjoy their work. The other good point about the shepherd is that properly trained ones will actually *stop* attacking if you tell them to.

If you like German shepherds, check out: Two other prime examples of German leadership in the field of scary-ass dog development, the Doberman pinscher and Rottweiler.

Weight: *50–80 pounds (22.5–36 kg).* **Height:** *21–24 inches (53.3–61 cm).* **Build:** *Graceful, well-proportioned body.* **Coat:** *Long, silky, gold or cream-colored hair.* **Brains:** *A well-bred golden is a highly intelligent, trainable animal. However, this breed is so popular that the gene pool has gotten rather shallow in places. Irresponsibly bred animals can sometimes be aggressive (a true rarity for goldens) or, more often, breathtakingly stupid.* **Bladder Matters:** *No special house-training problems.*

The Incredible Origin: For decades it was bruited about that the golden retriever was descended from Russian circus dogs. In fact, it was probably created in nineteenth-century Scotland by interbreeding various types of setters and spaniels over several generations. Originally developed as a hunting dog (and still used that way in some quarters), it is today one of the world's most popular companion breeds and the default pet of choice for suburban, middle-class, cul-de-sac-dwelling families everywhere.

Trademark Traits: A well-bred golden is an ideal family dog. Intelligent, easy to train, and eager to please, it is a loyal friend to both children and adults. Carefully bred dogs of this variety are almost completely devoid of aggression, and they possess a keen intelligence that makes them invaluable as guide and search dogs. Their physical attractiveness doesn't hurt their cachet, either.

Headaches and Hassles: Goldens can be quite spastic up until their second or third birthdays, after which they settle down and become merely "exuberant." Obedience training is definitely a must, unless you relish the prospect of shouting "Down, Piper, *down!*" dozens of times a day. Goldens love to eat and will gain weight easily if overindulged or not exercised properly. They also shed copiously.

Special Perks: Golden retrievers require regular exercise, but this can be accomplished with minimal fuss simply by playing fetch. The typical golden will indulge in this game all day—or until its owner gets tired of palming a spit-soaked tennis ball. They get along well with other dogs and with cats, which, in their enthusiasm at meeting a new friend, they may cover with slobber. *Anything* a golden retriever really likes will eventually wind up

L	⤬∞

DOG TRAITS

WHO SHOULD GET THIS DOG?

A properly trained and adequately exercised golden can live in a country mansion or a city apartment. Though too exuberant for very young kids and the elderly, it's perfect for active singles and families with older children. It has few vices, save for messiness and hyperactivity.

OWNER TRAITS

covered with slobber. These dogs love water and mud, and they won't pass up an opportunity to become absolutely filthy. Whether this is a "Special Perk" or "Headache and Hassle" depends on your idea of recreation.

Bugs in the System: Goldens like to carry things in their mouths. They like it so much that some could be accused of having oral fixations. They may trot around for hours holding a slobber-soaked stick, a shoe, or an interesting piece of underwear they found on the bedroom floor. They may make a point of presenting said underwear to houseguests.

If someone broke into my house, this dog would: Wag its tail and grin like an idiot. Goldens are about as useful for home defense as an Amish bodyguard. Some *may* bark to announce the arrival of an intruder. Many won't.

If you like golden retrievers, check out: That *other* ruler of the suburbs, the Labrador retriever. If you want something a bit smaller, there's always the ever-happy cocker spaniel.

Gordon Setter

Weight: 45–75 pounds (20.3–33.8 kg). *Height:* 23–27 inches (58.4–68.6 cm). *Build:* Muscular and sleek. *Coat:* Flat, silky, medium-length hair, in black with tan accents. *Brains:* Intelligent, but can be rather immature and somewhat difficult to train. Positive reinforcement is pretty much the only way to go. Socialization at an early age will keep the dog from becoming excessively shy. *Bladder Matters:* No particular house-training problems.

The Incredible Origin: Developed in early nineteenth-century England by the duke of Gordon, this breed is one of the largest and strongest of the various setters. It is very much a working dog—so much so that it may have trouble adjusting to home life.

Trademark Traits: The Gordon enjoys the company of its family but can be cool to strangers—though it will accept an occasional pat on the head without complaint. They can also be particularly fond of, and patient with, children. Gordons have an extremely long fuse; it takes a great deal to make them angry.

Headaches and Hassles: Gordon setters are big "talkers" and can develop a wide retinue of howls, barks, and whines to signify everything from the approach of strangers to the fact that their water bowl is empty. Because they can be easily distracted by strange scents, they can never be allowed off their lead in public. An energetic breed, the Gordon needs regular walks and off-leash romps in a fenced area. As with so many other breeds, if this one doesn't receive the exercise and attention it requires, the Gordon setter may vent its frustrations on your home and property. Also, it may be aggressive around other dogs.

Special Perks: The Gordon's coat isn't all that high maintenance, requiring only regular brushings to keep it in good condition.

Bugs in the System: This breed is generally healthy, but some may suffer from bloat, hip dysplasia, and hypothyroidism.

If someone broke into my house, this dog would: Announce his arrival by barking, then promptly fall back asleep.

If you like the Gordon setter, check out: The hunting world's ultimate glamour puss, the Irish setter.

DOG TRAITS

WHO SHOULD GET THIS DOG?

A family or individual with the time and inclination to provide the exercise and training the Gordon needs. Also, patience would be a very good trait. Gordons aren't all that common, so it may take up to a year to secure a well-bred puppy.

OWNER TRAITS

Great Dane

Weight: 110–175 pounds (49.5–78.8 kg). **Height:** 31–36 inches (78.7–91.4 cm). **Build:** Powerful but sleek. **Coat:** Extremely short hair, in colors ranging from fawn to black to "harlequin" (white with black spots). **Brains:** Smart and amenable to training. **Bladder Matters:** No particular house-training issues.

The Incredible Origin: It must gall the Germans to hear this beast called the Great Dane. This mighty dog is as much a product of Germany as BMWs and soulless techno-pop. First displayed there in the mid-nineteenth century (and called, tellingly, the *Deutsche Dogge*), it was used for everything from big-game hunting to guard work. The "Dane" was chosen as Germany's national dog in 1876, and Chancellor Otto von Bismarck himself kept them as pets and bodyguards.

Trademark Traits: The original Danes could be savage killers, but decades of controlled breeding have made them much more civilized. Today's model wants nothing more than to hang out with its family and in general is quite lovable. However, this dog is *huge*, so if you want to control it, obedience classes are essential. Teaching must begin early, while the dog is still relatively small. It is very important to establish your dominance at this time. It is also important to socialize the dog and nip any aggressive tendencies in the bud. This canine can *already* be rather territorial and protective. You don't need to encourage it.

Headaches and Hassles: Danes, particularly puppies, can be very hard on your garden and other landscaping. Some drool. Indoors, they can cause epic damage to everything from beds to carpeting. Danes also cost a lot to keep—more for food, for veterinary bills, etc. They can be aggressive toward other dogs and problematic around cats. Finally, for the entire time you own the dog, every single stranger you pass on the street will say either "Who's leading who?" or "You ought to put a saddle on him!"

DOG TRAITS

WHO SHOULD GET THIS DOG?

Someone with experience handling a large canine—and who doesn't have very young children. The Great Dane isn't necessarily aggressive. It's just that it's so large and a child is so small, there are bound to be collisions. This can be a particular problem with exuberant puppies.

OWNER TRAITS

Special Perks: Regular brushing keeps a Great Dane neat and clean, which is a good thing because bathing them is akin to washing a car. The breed responds well to consistent, positive training.

Bugs in the System: Danes can be afflicted with hip dysplasia, heart problems, and certain cancers. Their short coats offer only minimal protection against winter weather. They also suffer terribly from bloat. *It is very important that you discuss this issue, and how to avoid it, with your vet.*

If someone broke into my house, this dog would: The mere sight of a Great Dane is enough to make most housebreakers turn tail. However, while this breed will almost certainly bark at intruders (again, this is usually all that's required) they can't be counted on to do anything else. Some, depending on their individual temperament, may attack. Others may not.

If you like the Great Dane, check out: The mighty mastiff—one of the Dane's most prominent ancestors. For a similar look and attitude in a smaller package, try the boxer.

Weight: 100–125 pounds (45–56.3 kg). *Height:* 27–32 inches (68.6–81.3 cm). *Build:* Massive, powerful body. *Coat:* Thick, long, white hair. *Brains:* Above-average intelligence. *Bladder Matters:* This dog urinates buckets, but that shouldn't be an issue since the Pyrenees presents no special house-training issues.

The Incredible Origin: For generations this dog served as a guardian of livestock in the Pyrenees Mountains along the border of France and Spain. But since at least the eighteenth century its good looks— including a snow-white coat that makes it resemble a bleached-out Newfoundland (to which it is related)— have won it a place of honor everywhere from the French royal court to American suburbia.

Trademark Traits: The Great Pyrenees's showstoppingly distinctive looks turn heads, but its personality and physical traits make it even more remarkable. It is the canine version of Mr. Right: An overwhelmingly powerful, deeply intimidating guardian with a dependable, loyal, loving personality (not to mention expressive eyes and the ability to listen, at great length, to whatever you care to vent about). They're good with children, guests, even other dogs. They will also tolerate cats, if socialized to them at an early age. The only way the average Pyrenees could hurt its master is if it fell on him or her.

Headaches and Hassles: The Pyrenees's coat is thicker and more tightly woven than a Persian rug. This offered great protection when the dog presided over flocks on high mountain plateaus, but might be considered overkill in Georgia in July. Since the dog essentially wears a parka year-round, its enthusiasm for, and tolerance of, outdoor physical activity flags greatly in summer. By the way, prepare yourself to see wads of this hair plastered to furniture and rolling tumbleweed-like across the living room floor. Also, during exercise the dog develops great, ropy strands of slobber at the corners of its mouth. To keep things from getting too gross, owners often bring along paper towels or a cloth diaper to dab the drool during walks. These sensitive dogs take bad experiences very much to heart, so the only way to train them is

DOG TRAITS

WHO SHOULD GET THIS DOG?
Families and individuals willing to provide the attention and grooming it requires. Given its cold-weather-friendly design, it would also help if you lived in Minnesota rather than, say, Miami. A backyard is a plus. This dog needs exercise, but lacks the stamina (especially in summer) to be a jogging partner.

OWNER TRAITS

by positive reinforcement. But even if you play nice, they can still be somewhat stubborn and resistant to training. Last but not least, we should mention this breed's colossal bowel movements. How would you feel about having a full-grown man crapping in your backyard? With a dog like the Pyrenees, that's what you'll face.

Special Perks: This dog is an awesome physical specimen, and its white fur makes it the center of attention wherever it goes. The Pyrenees's obvious sturdiness (its back is as wide as a coffee table) makes its gentle personality even more endearing.

Bugs in the System: In a strange twist of genetics, the Pyrenees has double dewclaws on its paws. These appear to perform no useful function. Because of its massive build, this dog is prone to skeletal problems, particularly as it ages. Also, its life span can be fairly short. Ten years is a very good run.

If someone broke into my house, this dog would: Issue a deep, dangerous-sounding bark that is usually enough, all by itself, to make the average intruder lose all interest in intruding. Should he be foolish enough to force a confrontation with this highly territorial breed, it will be over before you can say, "emergency room."

If you like the Great Pyrenees, check out: The Newfoundland and Saint Bernard, both of which are equally tough and immune to cold weather. As an added bonus, the Newfoundland is also waterproof (see page 142).

Weight: 85–140 pounds (38.3–63 kg). *Height:* 24–29 inches (59.7–72.4 cm). *Build:* Large and powerful. *Coat:* Short hair with tricolor markings. *Brains:* Smart but sometimes stubborn. They respond fairly well to positive training but not at all to punishment. *Bladder Matters:* This breed can take seven to nine months to completely house-train.

The Incredible Origin: Allegedly developed in Switzerland and originally used as an all-purpose farm dog (it did everything from pull carts to guard flocks), the "Swissy" teetered on the brink of extinction at the dawn of the twentieth century. During World War II, when the dog was used as a draft animal by the Swiss army, there were no more than perhaps 400. Since then, careful breeding has steadily increased its numbers.

Trademark Traits: Swissies are devoted to their families but not particularly interested in anyone or anything else. As with other large, intimidating-looking breeds, they aren't overtly aggressive but will stand their ground when confronted by a stranger.

Headaches and Hassles: A typical Swissy can demolish a 40-pound bag of food each and every week. They also shed, particularly in spring and fall.

Special Perks: If socialized early to cats and other dogs, the typical Swissy can share its domain without problems. These dogs may be large, but they don't require an immense amount of exercise. Regular walks and backyard play dates will suffice.

Bugs in the System: Problems include hip and elbow dysplasia, bloat, epilepsy, and eye difficulties. Not surprisingly, Swissies don't do well in hot weather.

If someone broke into my house, this dog would: Sound the alarm. This breed makes an excellent watchdog, because it quickly notices any change in its environment and responds by barking. If pressed, this massive dog will also defend its family.

If you like the Greater Swiss mountain dog, check out: Another burly product of Switzerland, the Bernese mountain dog.

XL	🛡	🐾
	DOG TRAITS	

WHO SHOULD GET THIS DOG?

A family or individual with a fenced backyard who can cater to the physical, monetary, and training needs of a very large breed. This is too much dog for the elderly or for families with small children.

OWNER TRAITS

Greyhound

*Weight: 60–70 pounds (27–31.5 kg). **Height:** 26–30 inches (66–76.2 cm). **Build:** Lithe, muscular, and extremely graceful. **Coat:** Very short hair in colors ranging from black to red to brindle, any of which can be mixed with white. Interestingly, they aren't available in gray. **Brains:** Above-average intellect. **Bladder Matters:** No special house-training problems. Rescue greyhounds are usually kennel trained.*

The Incredible Origin: Lean, lithe, greyhoundlike dogs have been a part of human society for eons. The classic model (sometimes called the English greyhound) is one of many varieties to bear the name, including Hungarian, Polish, Sicilian, and Spanish models. Since time immemorial this particular type of dog has been used to run down game animals—a job for which it is ideal. Today they are used primarily for the despicable sport of dog racing. In fact, most owners acquire their animals from rescue services that try to place "retired" racers in good homes.

Trademark Traits: Greyhounds are a bizarre mix of explosive athleticism and indolence. Though they can outrun almost anything on four legs, they are quite content to lie quietly around the house for hours on end. They enjoy car rides and don't require enormous amounts of food. They are tolerant of older, respectful children, nearly silent, loving yet undemanding, and their short, neat coats require next to no grooming. Why are they such pussycats? Perhaps, experts suggest, because these former racing dogs are just so darn grateful to have loved ones and a home.

Headaches and Hassles: Some greyhounds suffer from separation anxiety. The best cure for this is to spend more time with them or get a second dog. Greyhounds may also take an unhealthy interest in small, furry things that resemble prey (such as, for instance, your cat). Likewise, a greyhound that sees a small, running animal will almost certainly pursue it. And since these dogs can reach 45 mph (72.4 kph), it will almost certainly catch it. For this reason it can never be trusted off its lead in public. Some females can become very maternal with human children, even disciplining them with a nip if they become (in the dog's opinion) too rambunctious. For obvious reasons, you will want to firmly dis-courage this behavior.

Special Perks: Greyhounds make excellent jogging partners—if you don't mind having the sort of jogging partner who, when you're doubled over, gasp-ing from exertion, isn't even breathing heavily. This dog needs several brisk walk/runs a week, plus a couple of chances to play, off-lead, in a large, high-fenced enclosure. After this they will be more than happy to go home, find a comfortable spot, and crash.

Bugs in the System: The greyhound is relatively free of genetic ailments. However, because of their short coats and lean bodies, they don't do well in cold weather without a coat.

If someone broke into my house, this dog would: Do nothing—unless the intruder was a rabbit. Then it would be in trouble.

If you like greyhounds, check out: The saluki, another very fast sight hound. However, it requires more grooming and can be harder to train.

Weight: *40–60 pounds (18–27 kg).* **Height:** *19–21 inches (48.3–53.3 cm).* **Build:** *Lithe and muscular.* **Coat:** *Very short hair, in a mix of black, orange, and white.* **Brains:** *Intelligent, but this breed is easily distracted.* **Bladder Matters:** *No special house-training problems.*

The Incredible Origin: Developed in England for pursuing hares, this old breed looks like a biggie-sized beagle—which it might well be. The harrier possesses the beagle's acute sense of smell, with the addition of the speed and the long legs necessary to keep up with fleet-footed game.

Trademark Traits: Harriers are very social and want to be with their owners as much as possible. If they're home alone, they may freak out from loneliness and frustration and "renovate" your interior decor. The best way to avoid this problem is to get another dog for them to play with.

Headaches and Hassles: This breed has been a field dog for most of its history. It was only recently (like, in the last 50 years) that anyone entertained the prospect of keeping it as a house pet. The hunting instinct is still very strong in the typical harrier, which means it may take off after interesting scents, whether you want it to or not. This breed needs a secure, fenced yard and must always be kept on a lead in public. Harriers also like to dig, and they may tunnel under a fence if given the chance. They love to eat and will become fat if overindulged. Finally, some tend to be "talkative," emitting a plaintive howl at odd times.

Special Perks: The harrier loves kids, loves adults, pretty much loves everybody. It gets along well with other dogs and can be easily socialized to cats. Their short coats require minimal grooming, though they do shed moderately.

Bugs in the System: Harriers are usually healthy and long-lived. However, hip dysplasia is sometimes a problem.

If someone broke into my house, this dog would: Announce the visitor with a sonorous bark/howl. But if the visitor is unwelcome, driving him off is up to you.

If you like the harrier, check out: The docile beagle.

DOG TRAITS

WHO SHOULD GET THIS DOG?

A family or individual with a fenced yard and the time to devote to training and exercise. No apartment dwellers, please. Be advised that this traditional hunting dog isn't the easiest (or even the tenth-easiest) animal to acclimate to domestic life. Before acquiring one, speak with a current harrier owner or responsible breeder.

OWNER TRAITS

Weight: 55–75 pounds (24.8–33.8 kg). **Height:** 24–28 inches (61–71.1 cm). **Build:** Muscular and graceful. **Coat:** Long, flowing, reddish hair. **Brains:** Difficult to train, because like many hunting dogs it is easily distracted. However a kind, consistent owner can usually get the job done. **Bladder Matters:** No particular house-training problems.

The Incredible Origin: This breed (once popularly known as "The Red Dog") has been used for centuries to locate birds—first for netting, later for shooting. Among outdoors enthusiasts it is prized for its scenting, pointing, and retrieving skills. That's why, when you take it for a walk, it usually keeps its nose to the ground, sweeping back and forth to cover the maximum amount of acreage. You may just be taking a turn around the block, but the Irish setter is doing what it was genetically programmed to do—looking for game. Though still an effective hunting companion, its good looks have made it a show-ring staple. It was allegedly crossed with the borzoi to give it its current, streamlined shape.

Trademark Traits: Exuberance, thy name is Irish setter. Full of energy and bounce, this breed is famous for its playfulness and overwhelming love of its family. This dog cannot be ignored or warehoused in the backyard. Irish setters demand attention and will suffer (as will you) if denied it. Also, not unlike another famous redhead, Lucille Ball, they can get into a spectacular amount of trouble.

Headaches and Hassles: Some have used words like "unmanageable" and even "crazy" to describe their setters. In fact, most problems arise because owners are "inexperienced." These dogs are extremely energetic and need lots of exercise. Not 20 minutes alone in the backyard, but long walks, plus supervised runs in fenced areas. Back when it was used primarily for hunting, this dog was famous for its endurance. If you don't find a way to burn that energy, then your setter may indeed become "crazy." Like other hunting dogs, this breed is easily distracted and can't be trusted off its lead in public. Plus, if your canine gets anywhere near the woods, budget some post-romp time to comb and clip all the burrs out of its silky coat. This dog can also be somewhat

DOG TRAITS

WHO SHOULD GET THIS DOG?

No apartment dwellers need apply. This dog definitely needs a fenced yard. A passel of older children is also a plus, to help it burn off energy. Whoever adopts it, whether a family or single, must be prepared to spend a great deal of time on exercise and training.

OWNER TRAITS

clumsy indoors, knocking over things and, sometimes, people. (Families with toddlers, please take note.)

Special Perks: It's extremely family-oriented and a good dog with children. The fact that it's one of the world's most beautiful canines doesn't hurt its rep, either. And if you enjoy playing fetch, you've just found your soul mate.

Bugs in the System: Problems include hip dysplasia, epilepsy, progressive retinal atrophy, bloat, and severe skin allergies. The typical setter may retain its rambunctious "puppy personality" for several years.

If someone broke into my house, this dog would: Bark, at a minimum. Irish setters are energetic barkers. Whether they would do anything besides bark is an open question. Some might take on an intruder, but some (probably most) wouldn't.

If you like the Irish setter, check out: That other supermodel of the hunting dog world, the golden retriever.

Weight: 23–30 pounds (10.4–13.5 kg). **Height:** 15–19 inches (38.1–48.3 cm). **Build:** Muscular and agile. **Coat:** Short and wiry hair, usually red. **Brains:** Intelligent, but like most terriers somewhat difficult to train and keep trained. **Bladder Matters:** No special house-training problems.

The Incredible Origin: Developed in Ireland and refined to its present form during the nineteenth century, this little dog is every bit the stereotypical Irishman—tough, combative, and sporting more bright red hair than the entire cast of *Riverdance*. It is allegedly closely related to the wirehaired fox terrier.

Trademark Traits: This dog's well-earned nicknames include the "red devil." It was famous for pursuing its quarry relentlessly. But though highly pugnacious in dogfights and when hunting everything from fox to badger, it is surprisingly even-tempered around humans.

Headaches and Hassles: The typical Irish terrier loves two things above all else: being with its master and fighting every dog it sees. You'll need to address this, repeatedly, during obedience training (the fighting, not the unconditional love). They typically don't like cats much either, and they can't be trusted around small furry creatures such as gerbils and hamsters. In public these dogs must always be leashed.

Special Perks: This is one of those very special dogs that will go to the mat for you, anytime, anywhere.

Bugs in the System: Though a generally healthy breed, it can suffer from a hereditary urinary condition, as well as eye disorders and foot problems.

If someone broke into my house, this dog would: Raise a furious racket, and then, in spite of the fact that it would probably weigh less than the intruder's leg, attack.

If you like the Irish terrier, check out: The equally lively but much more common fox terrier. Or the smaller but just as perky cairn terrier.

DOG TRAITS

WHO SHOULD GET THIS DOG?

The Irish terrier has lots of energy, but that energy can be expended with regular walks and backyard romps. It's a good choice for families with older children, active singles, and even seniors. Just remember that this dog will see itself as a family member, not a pet.

OWNER TRAITS

Irish Wolfhound

Weight: 110–125+ pounds (49.5–56+ kg). **Height:** *28–38 inches (71.1–96.5 cm).* **Build:** *Very tall, well-muscled, and graceful.* **Coat:** *Coarse, rough hair in colors ranging from red to gray to black to white.* **Brains:** *Accepts training, but can sometimes be obstinate. Responds best to positive reinforcement.* **Bladder Matters:** *No particular house-training problems.*

The Incredible Origin: Developed in Ireland to, as the name suggests, take out wolves, this breed literally hunted itself out of a job. The wolfhound was almost extinct when nineteenth-century English breeders revived it. Today this tallest of all canines makes an excellent lapdog—if you're Paul Bunyan.

Trademark Traits: For a dog designed to kill wolves, the typical wolfhound is certainly mellow. Comfortable with other dogs and easy (though somewhat reserved) with strangers, all it wants to do is spend quiet evenings at home with its family. Some, if properly socialized, get along well with cats. Some don't. It's up to the individual dog and how much prey drive they retain.

Headaches and Hassles: Like other hounds that hunt by sight, the Irish wolfhound is easily distracted. If it sees a squirrel or other small (or not-so-small) fleeing animal, it will take off in pursuit. For that reason it must always be leashed in public. Its yard should also include a high fence. Invisible fences are useless, because a dog as big and fast as a wolfhound can run right through them. Do not, during puppyhood, allow a wolfhound to get in the habit of jumping on people. This is annoying with most breeds, but it's a nightmare with an animal that, when standing, can look a grown man in the eye. Also this puts too much stress on its skeleton and muscles.

Special Perks: The wolfhound's coat looks like a nightmare to maintain, but all that's required is regular brushings. They shed, but don't "blow their coats" in spring and fall, as do so many other types. This dog can also be as athletic or as sedentary as you'd like it to be. If you want to go for walks, it's there (be advised, however, that very young dogs can sustain joint damage from prolonged

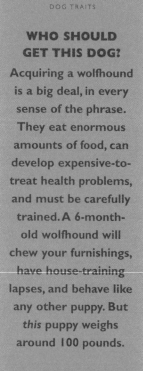

XL

DOG TRAITS

WHO SHOULD GET THIS DOG?

Acquiring a wolfhound is a big deal, in every sense of the phrase. They eat enormous amounts of food, can develop expensive-to-treat health problems, and must be carefully trained. A 6-month-old wolfhound will chew your furnishings, have house-training lapses, and behave like any other puppy. But *this* puppy weighs around 100 pounds.

OWNER TRAITS

exertion); if you want to sack out on the sofa, it's there, too. Trouble is, only one of you may be able to lie there at once.

Bugs in the System: The wolfhound paid a terrible price for its size. These dogs only live an average of six to eight years and are subject to a long, long list of hereditary disorders, including, but not confined to bloat, heart disease (a very serious problem), cancer, hypothyroidism, hip dysplasia, malformations of the joint cartilage, eye disorders, and seizures. *Because wolfhounds have so many problems, obtain one only from a careful, top-notch breeder.* Also, locate a veterinarian with experience caring for the breed—and reconcile yourself to the fact that this dog can be very expensive to maintain. You might even want to purchase a doggie health insurance policy. Seriously.

If someone broke into my house, this dog would: Do little if anything. Although the mere sight of an Irish wolfhound is enough to make the average intruder dirty his drawers, these dogs are generally quite placid. If provoked, however (and it usually takes quite a lot to do this), they *may* defend their homes and families.

If you like the Irish wolfhound, check out: The Scottish deerhound, which offers the look of the wolfhound in a (slightly) smaller package.

Weight: 7–15 pounds (3.2–6.8 kg). Height: 13–15 inches (33–38 cm). Build: Remarkably slim and fragile-looking. Coat: Very short hair, in colors ranging from black to red to cream. Brains: Intelligent but often stubborn and easily distracted during training. Bladder Matters: Can be difficult to house-train.

The Incredible Origin: This tiny specimen is a toy greyhound, developed as a plaything for European aristocracy but also fully capable of hunting small game. Though common throughout southern Europe during the Middle Ages, it was a particular favorite in Italy—hence the name. The Italian greyhound can reach speeds of 40 mph (64.3 kph)—more than enough to chase down a rabbit at full sprint. Although sometimes still used for hunting, its natural habitat is on a rug by the fireplace. That's not surprising, since these spindly little animals carry about as much body fat as your average broiled, skinless chicken breast.

Trademark Traits: Unlike many toy breeds, the Italian is fairly placid. It gets along with respectful, older children, other dogs, and even cats, and it can be playful with its immediate family. The dog is so emotional, however, that the slightest disturbance with its owner can set it to shivering.

Headaches and Hassles: Like most hounds, the Italian is easily distracted or spooked. If it sees something interesting, it will pursue it (or run from it). Some have even leapt off apartment balconies because they spotted their owners on the street. For this reason it must always be kept on a lead in public (and off of balconies). It tends to mature quite slowly, and it may still display exuberant "puppy behavior" into its third and fourth years. This sensitive little companion requires ample love and attention—so much that it's regularly described as "needy." For obvious reasons, the Italian greyhound doesn't fare well in the cold, so stock up on doggie sweaters. This breed is also fairly fragile and prone to broken legs.

Special Perks: If given proper exercise, Italians can live in accommodations ranging from apartments to mansions. They are very neat and easy to keep clean. Though they *can* bark, they seldom

DOG TRAITS

WHO SHOULD GET THIS DOG?

A calm individual or family that can provide this somewhat skittish breed the loving warmth and reassurance it needs to stay on an even keel. Not a good choice for families with rambunctious children.

OWNER TRAITS

do, and almost never to excess. If properly socialized, they can live with cats and other dogs.

Bugs in the System: Italians can be very long-lived. A life span of 15 to 18 years isn't unusual. However, some suffer from (among other things) hypothyroidism, seizure disorders, eye problems, and luxated patellae (dislocated knee joints). They are also vulnerable to (and display an extreme dislike of) foul weather. Good luck getting your Italian to go outdoors on a rainy, blustery day.

If someone broke into my house, this dog would: Bark when the stranger approached, then stand around looking worried while the stranger unplugged your TV and carried it away. These dogs are very big on standing around looking worried.

If you like the Italian greyhound, check out: The marginally sturdier whippet, or the full-size greyhound.

Weight: 15–18 pounds (6.8–8.1 kg). *Height:* 10–15 inches (25.4–38.1 cm). *Build:* Compact and powerful. Leg length and body shape can vary widely from dog to dog. *Coat:* Jacks are available in short-haired, wirehaired, and "broken" (a combination of the two) varieties. The coat is mostly white, with black, tan, and/or brown mixed in. *Brains:* Exceptionally intelligent. A patient, competent owner can teach it a wide array of tricks. *Bladder Matters:* No special house-training problems.

The Incredible Origin: The Jack Russell was developed by a nineteenth-century English parson named . . . well, you can guess his name. Designed for putting the hurt to small game, this dog was for decades refused recognition by breed associations because its physical makeup (every hairstyle short of a Mohawk and massive variations in leg length and head shape) made it difficult to classify. The version recognized by the American Kennel Club is called the Parson Russell terrier.

Trademark Traits: Jacks are breathtakingly intelligent, possess vivacious personalities, and are awesomely athletic. Unfortunately, they are also possibly the most high-tempered and truculent of all terriers, which is saying quite a bit. As anyone who has dealt with this breed can tell you, their nicknames, including "Pocket Pit Bull" and "Jack Russell Terrorist" are well deserved.

Headaches and Hassles: Though it's comparatively tiny, the Jack's strong personality may lead it to challenge and even dominate a weak-willed owner. It will also attack small animals such as rats, squirrels, and birds if given half the chance and will fight other dogs—including those twenty times its size. Firm training and careful socialization can, in many cases, mitigate this behavior, but the typical Jack can't be trusted off its lead in public. Also, this canine's Olympic-caliber athletic skills (they can, among other things, jump higher than most people's shoulders) mean that if so moved, they can easily escape from supposedly "dog-proofed" yards.

A bored or ignored Jack may develop a passion for barking or digging. Actually, truth be told, even a well-adjusted dog may still engage in recreational digging and raise a ruckus whenever someone approaches the front door.

DOG TRAITS

WHO SHOULD GET THIS DOG?

An experienced dog enthusiast—preferably someone who has handled terriers. Remember, *this dog isn't for everyone.* A Jack will push around a milquetoast owner, so if the words "mild-mannered" or "passive" have ever been associated with your personality, this is *not* the canine companion for you.

OWNER TRAITS

Special Perks: In the hands of a firm owner, the Jack is both a loving family pet and an amusing source of entertainment—not to mention a very effective burglar alarm. They can even (as proven by Moose, the dog that played Eddie on the sitcom *Frasier*) learn to sit still and behave. If you get on their good side, you'll find them capable of mastering almost any behavior.

Bugs in the System: Some are prone to eye diseases, deafness, kneecap dislocations, and hip joint problems.

If someone broke into my house, this dog would: Attack ferociously, without regard for its opponent's size or its own safety. Jacks are devoted to their families and will defend them to the bitter end.

If you like Jack Russell terriers, check out: The fox terrier, which though larger than the Jack, is arguably less of a handful. Or the merry, energetic, and slightly smaller cairn terrier.

Keeshond

Weight: *50–65 pounds (22.5–29.3 kg).* **Height:** *16–19 inches (40.6–48.3 cm).* **Build:** *Stocky.* **Coat:** *Thick double coat, usually in gray and black.* **Brains:** *Intelligent and fairly easy to train.* **Bladder Matters:** *No particular house-training problems.*

The Incredible Origin: During an eighteenth-century political dispute this spitzlike dog (used primarily as a house pet and guardian of river barges) had the misfortune of becoming the mascot for the losing side in a rebellion against the Dutch royal house. Its name is even derived from the rebel leader, Cornelius "Kees" de Gyzelaar. Not surprisingly, this canine suddenly became very unfashionable once the king got his throne back. Today the keeshond is quite popular, even though Holland, perhaps as a final slight, doesn't recognize it as a purebred.

Trademark Traits: This breed is a bit more mellow and easy to live with than other spitz-type canines such as the Samoyed—perhaps because it was created not to pull sleds, but to serve as a house pet and guardian.

Headaches and Hassles: The keeshond's heavy coat requires daily combing, and during spring and fall it comes out in clumps. The dog should be socialized to people and strange situations as a puppy, so that its natural caution doesn't turn into paranoia. It needs lots of company and may suffer from separation anxiety if left alone too long. Keeshonds can also become hair-trigger barkers.

Special Perks: Cheerful and even-tempered, the keeshond treasures its family and thrives on companionship. This breed usually gets along well with cats and other dogs. It's also good with strangers, though not so good that it becomes an ineffective watchdog.

Bugs in the System: Generally healthy, but sometimes subject to eye disorders, hip dysplasia, and heart defects.

If someone broke into my house, this dog would: Bark like crazy. No one sneaks up on a keeshond.

If you like the keeshond, check out: The schipperke, yet another breed that got its start guarding Low Country riverboats.

DOG TRAITS

WHO SHOULD GET THIS DOG?

An individual or family willing to provide the attention it loves. Keeshonds can be a bit emotional, becoming upset by too much noise or too many arguments. A placid family situation or a low-key single owner is always best.

OWNER TRAITS

Weight: 33–40 pounds (14.9–18 kg). **Height:** 18–20 inches (45.7–50.8 cm). **Build:** Sturdy and muscular. **Coat:** Thick, silky, usually bluish-gray coat. **Brains:** Extremely intelligent, but like many terriers can be resistant to training. **Bladder Matters:** No special house-training issues.

The Incredible Origin: This dog was developed in Ireland as a hunter and herder. It was even allegedly harnessed to butter churns. It is named after County Kerry in Ireland, in spite of the fact that it has no particular connection to the area.

Trademark Traits: The Kerry is filled with vigor, intelligence, and lots of attitude. These athletic dogs love their families and can be remarkably good with respectful children.

Headaches and Hassles: The Kerry's smart-looking coat requires extensive home care and regular professional grooming (its standard haircut features a facial trim that reminds one of Prince during his Revolution days). Let one loose in the woods and every burr and twig within a 10-mile radius will adhere to its coat. Also, its fetching beard soaks up a great deal of dog-dish water, which it will then distribute like a soaker hose around the house. The Kerry is good with people but can be very, very bad with other dogs—and cats and other small animals, for that matter. For this reason it must always be kept leashed in public. These dogs are dominant by nature and will test a wishy-washy owner.

Special Perks: The Kerry's coat may be high maintenance, but at least it doesn't shed. This dog is also devoted to its owner, whom it will follow around all day like a shadow.

Bugs in the System: Problems include hip dysplasia, flea allergies, cysts, and immune system and blood disorders.

If someone broke into my house, this dog would: Raise the alarm with furious barking and then, if it felt its family was endangered, attack.

If you like the Kerry blue terrier, check out: The Airedale, featuring all the attitude of the Kerry blue but with a slightly less expensive haircut.

DOG TRAITS

WHO SHOULD GET THIS DOG?

A family or individual with the strong personality needed to control a strong-willed dog. Also, someone with deep pockets. The Kerry can soak up around $70 each month in grooming costs alone.

OWNER TRAITS

Komondor

Weight: 80–135 pounds (36–60.8 kg). *Height:* 23–32 inches (58.4–81.3 cm). *Build:* Muscular and extremely powerful. *Coat:* Long, white cords. *Brains:* Intelligent and easily trainable by an authoritative master. *Bladder Matters:* No special house-training problems.

The Incredible Origin: This old Hungarian breed served as a guardian of herds, putting the hurt to wolves, bears, and anything else intent on enjoying an unauthorized lamb dinner. Today it's mostly a family pet, though some American ranchers still use these bizarre-looking dogs to protect sheep from coyotes.

Trademark Traits: The komondor may look like something created by the Children's Television Workshop, but it's definitely a serious dog. The breed is suspicious of strangers, steady in the face of danger, not particularly affectionate, and capable of messing up troublemakers of any species.

Headaches and Hassles: Komondors need lots of exercise, and they can cause extensive destruction if bored. Their coat takes a lot of grooming, and it can soak up everything from rain to dog-bowl water. Komondors are deeply suspicious of human and animal strangers, and should be supervised in their presence. They can be highly energetic and boisterous. Translation: Keep them away from old people and very young kids.

Special Perks: This breed is one of the world's most unique. Well-bred, well-trained komondors are also well mannered in the house.

Bugs in the System: A healthy breed, it nevertheless can suffer from bloat and hip problems. For obvious reasons, they don't thrive in warm climates.

If someone broke into my house, this dog would: First warn off the troublemaker with a bark so deep it sounds like cannon fire. In a confrontation, it would bring to bear all the strength and speed it once used to fight wild predators. Komondors can be very protective of their owners, their owner's children, and even their owner's other *pets.*

If you like the komondor, check out: The puli, another dread-locked Hungarian breed that's roughly half the size of this one.

DOG TRAITS

WHO SHOULD GET THIS DOG?

Someone with a large yard, the personal strength to command such a big dog, and the time for careful training. It's worth noting that this dog was bred to work, not to wallow around the house. Unless you happen to have a herd of vulnerable sheep, the komondor probably isn't your best choice.

OWNER TRAITS

Weight: 80–110 pounds (36–49.5 kg). *Height:* 22–26 inches (55.9–66 cm). *Build:* Muscular and very sturdy. *Coat:* Long, thick, and white hair. *Brains:* Intelligent, but willful. Training can be a drawn-out process. *Bladder Matters:* No special house-training problems.

The Incredible Origin: This Hungarian breed was an all-purpose working dog, serving as a hunter and a guardian of both flocks and people (its name literally means "guard"). Used in Europe as police dogs, they've found employment in America and elsewhere guarding sheep on the open range, where they serve as the welcoming committee for marauding coyotes.

Trademark Traits: The kuvasz is the John Wayne of dogs—loyal, faithful, and steady, but not all that affectionate or demonstrative. This is not the sort of canine who will play Frisbee with you in the park. Naturally suspicious of strangers, it should be well-socialized as a puppy to keep it from becoming *too* suspicious.

Headaches and Hassles: The kuvasz's big, thick coat comes out in big, thick clumps come spring and fall. Daily brushing is required. It is extremely strong and energetic, which means long walks (and a secure, fenced yard) are a must. It may try to dominate a weak owner and can be aggressive toward strange animals and unfamiliar people. Finally, the kuvasz pays very close attention to outside goings-on and may herald each new sight and/or sound, no matter how insignificant, with a bone-rattling bark.

Special Perks: A well-socialized kuvasz is a devoted family guardian, and it can be especially protective of children. It can also adjust to living with other dogs and even cats, both of which it will consider part of its "flock."

Bugs in the System: Prone to hip dysplasia and eye problems.

If someone broke into my house, this dog would: Stand and fight, even if the "someone" was the Devil himself.

If you like the kuvasz, check out: The Great Pyrenees, another huge, snow-white guardian that's bigger, and perhaps less stand-offish, than the kuvasz.

DOG TRAITS

WHO SHOULD GET THIS DOG?
A family or individual with the energy and commitment necessary to manage a powerful, willful dog—a dog that, truth be told, would much prefer sitting out in a field guarding sheep to trotting around a suburban backyard.

OWNER TRAITS

Labrador Retriever

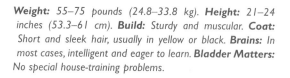

Weight: 55–75 pounds (24.8–33.8 kg). *Height:* 21–24 inches (53.3–61 cm). *Build:* Sturdy and muscular. *Coat:* Short and sleek hair, usually in yellow or black. *Brains:* In most cases, intelligent and eager to learn. *Bladder Matters:* No special house-training problems.

The Incredible Origin: Along with the golden retriever, the Labrador reigns as America's king of the cul-de-sac. A hunting breed developed from dogs allegedly used by Newfoundland fishermen to help haul in their nets, it is famous for its tracking skills, retrieving prowess, and "soft mouth" that enables it to fetch game without damaging it. This breed is also easily trained, even-tempered, and happy, making it an excellent pet—a fact not lost upon the hundreds of thousands of people who own it worldwide. The "Lab" is also used as everything from guide dog to narcotics sniffer. The British and North American versions have lately begun to diverge, however. The American dog runs a bit larger and is more muscular.

Trademark Traits: The same traits that made the Lab an excellent gun dog (patience and even temper) make it an excellent house pet. This big, energetic canine loves to play (especially in water) and adores its family.

Headaches and Hassles: The Lab can shed profusely, especially in spring and fall. This breed is full of energy and can go absolutely bonkers if it doesn't receive regular workouts. Be advised that if there is a pond, lake, stream, or mud puddle located anywhere in this dog's domain, it will find it and swim in it. While it is great with older kids, it might be too much for very young children. It can be spectacularly clumsy, especially when excited, clearing end tables with one sweep of its always-wagging tail, or knocking over grandpa with a careless shoulder to the shin. Careful training will help keep this exuberance in check. Some Labs can develop what can only be called oral fixations, carrying around a favorite toy, a shoe, or some other item from dawn to dusk. They will also overeat if given the chance.

DOG TRAITS

WHO SHOULD GET THIS DOG?

A family or individual who can meet its needs for exercise, guidance, and love. This dog must be a part of your life. About the only way to ruin a Lab's sunny disposition is to turn it out into the backyard and ignore it. Its size and clumsiness make it a poor fit for older people and very young children.

OWNER TRAITS

Special Perks: If there's a better companion for a boisterous, growing family, we haven't seen it. A well-socialized Lab will play with children until they drop from exhaustion. For a big dog it is also extraordinarily gentle. The only way it could hurt anyone is through awkwardness. Labs are also hardwired to play fetch. You will tire of throwing the ball long before the dog tires of bringing it back.

Bugs in the System: Hip and elbow dysplasia, along with several eye diseases. Because the Lab is so popular (and thus, so heavily bred), it is important to get a high-quality puppy from a careful breeder.

If someone broke into my house, this dog would: Grin and wag its tail. This is the breed's only major shortcoming. Most are useless as guardians.

If you like the Labrador retriever, check out: The official dog of bourgeois suburbanites everywhere—the golden retriever.

Weight: 12–18 pounds (5.4–8.1 kg). Height: 9–11 inches (22.9–27.9 cm). Build: Stocky and sturdy. Coat: Long, thick coat in a variety of colors. Brains: Intelligent and will accept training, but their strong constitutions can make teaching difficult. They want to know what's in it for them. Translation: Give them treats. Bladder Matters: Often difficult to house-train.

The Incredible Origin: This breed hails from Tibet, where it was used to guard palaces and Buddhist temples. (This is pretty remarkable, considering that the dog's eyes are barely visible under an avalanche of long, straight hair.) Often it worked in conjunction with the massive Tibetan mastiff. The Lhasa provided the bark, while the mastiff furnished the bite. In its homeland it is known as the *abso seng kye*, or "bark lion sentinel dog." The breed came to the United States in 1933 when a pair was given to an American couple by the Dalai Lama.

Trademark Traits: The Lhasa looks like a lapdog, but it has plenty of attitude. Bred as a temple guardian, it takes its role as a sentinel seriously. These dogs can be very strong willed, leery of unfamiliar people (to the point, in some cases, of attacking them), and tough-minded. They will make you earn their loyalty.

Headaches and Hassles: Believe it or not, this tiny breed will walk all over a weak owner. Also, it will take only so much teasing, or discipline, before it bites whomever is dishing it out. Lhasas can be highly suspicious of strangers and problematic with other dogs and cats. If they aren't well socialized as puppies, this distrustfulness can sour into paranoia. Their hair must be regularly combed or it will turn into a massive matted mess. If you don't have time for grooming (or if you'd just like to make eye contact with your dog occasionally), the Lhasa's long locks can be dispensed with in favor of a shorter utility cut. A poorly trained Lhasa may fly into violent tantrums if it doesn't get its way, and it can be prone to nuisance barking. Even a well-trained example of this breed can still display a lot of willfulness and "attitude." The dog is also an incurable snorer.

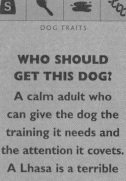

DOG TRAITS

WHO SHOULD GET THIS DOG?

A calm adult who can give the dog the training it needs and the attention it covets. A Lhasa is a terrible pet for families with small children. It is possessive of its toys and food bowl and will retaliate against even minor teasing or rough handling.

OWNER TRAITS

Special Perks: The Lhasa doesn't need much exercise. However, it does like to play and can make an adoring, fun, and energetic companion. It is hopelessly devoted to its owner—though it has little use for the rest of the human race.

Bugs in the System: This breed suffers from a number of problems, including skin and kidney disorders and respiratory conditions. The eyes are vulnerable both to injury and to genetic disorders such as corneal ulcers. Their ears require regular cleaning to avoid infections.

If someone broke into my house, this dog would: Go into a barking fit that would make Buddha proud. And if an invader persists, the tiny Lhasa is quite willing to brawl.

If you like the Lhasa apso, check out: A couple of other compact Asian imports, the Pekingese and Shih Tzu.

Weight: 4–6 pounds (1.8–2.7 kg). *Height:* 8–10 inches (20.3–25.4 cm). *Build:* Tiny and fragile. *Coat:* Long, silky, white hair. *Brains:* Intelligent and easy to train (except for the house-training issue). *Bladder Matters:* House-training can require more patience (and paper towels) than with other breeds.

The Incredible Origin: Dogs similar to the Maltese have been trotting around the Mediterranean world for thousands of years, mostly serving as pets for wealthy noblewomen. Today's version, which was perfected in the nineteenth century, still serves primarily as a bedtime foot warmer and post-date debriefing confidant. It is such a close relation of the bichon frise that it was once called the bichon Maltese. (No one is quite sure why, or even if, it came to be named after the Mediterranean island of Malta.)

Trademark Traits: This diminutive dog just wants to be adored. It's devoted to its owner, loves to cuddle, wants to sleep with you, and wouldn't mind being carried around all the waking hours of the day. Then again, the Maltese is so cute and animated, chances are you probably won't *mind* carrying it.

Headaches and Hassles: The breed's long, silky coat is both a glory (for the dog) and a curse (for you). To reach its full potential, it must be combed and brushed daily and washed regularly. You'll need special brushes and curlers. Its satiny head hair and bangs must be tied in a topknot so the dog can see, blah, blah, *blah.* Or you can let it go natural. Your dog will look like a rag mop, but it won't care. The Maltese can be somewhat possessive of its owner, hates being alone, and doesn't do well with very young children—which is a real problem, because many a breed guide states that it *does* get along with them. The difficulty is that the tiny tots are too rough on the dog, and the dog responds by being too rough on the *kids.* Such retaliation often lands these precious pooches in animal shelters. Maltese will also eat too much if given the chance. If you don't wipe its mouth after meals, the hair around it will discolor.

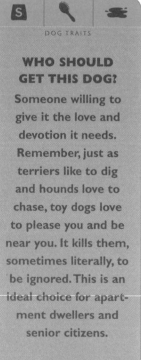

DOG TRAITS

WHO SHOULD GET THIS DOG?

Someone willing to give it the love and devotion it needs. Remember, just as terriers like to dig and hounds love to chase, toy dogs love to please you and be near you. It kills them, sometimes literally, to be ignored. This is an ideal choice for apartment dwellers and senior citizens.

OWNER TRAITS

Special Perks: This undemanding little dog needs only short strolls for exercise, supplemented with romps through the house. Actually all it *really* needs is to be near you. Better yet, the Maltese doesn't shed. So all those long, silky white hairs stay on the dog instead of on your clothing, furniture, and rugs.

Bugs in the System: Subject to various eye diseases. The eyes may also tear excessively, discoloring the fur beneath them if it is not cleaned regularly. Also, the spot in the center of the dog's back where its hair parts can easily become sunburned.

If someone broke into my house, this dog would: Greet him with furious barking. Be warned, however, that it may also greet the mail carrier the same way—every single day.

If you like the Maltese, check out: This breed's kissing cousin, the bichon frise. Or if you like a lapdog with a bit more fire, investigate the Lhasa Apso.

Mastiff

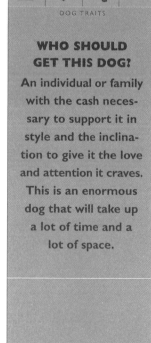

Weight: *Begins at 120 pounds and can exceed 200 (54–90+ kg).* **Height:** *26–36 inches (66–91.4 cm).* **Build:** *Massive.* **Coat:** *Short and tight hair, in brindles and fawns.* **Brains:** *Average intelligence, though some can be buttheads about training. Obedience class is mandatory.* **Bladder Matters:** *No particular house-training issues,*

The Incredible Origin: The mastiff (technically, the Old English mastiff) is said to be descended from dogs brought to England by Phoenician traders more than 2,500 years ago. It was originally a war and fighting dog, but today (in a much less aggressive form) serves as a guardian and companion animal. Is this breed's history really that old? We're not going to contest it. Not to the mastiff's face, anyway.

Trademark Traits: Well-bred examples of this lumbering beast are (thank God) even-tempered, trainable, and loving toward their families (particularly toward children). However, they retain enough of their old traits, and frightening looks, to make them extremely effective guardians.

Headaches and Hassles: This isn't a cheap dog to keep. A full-grown mastiff can hammer down 40 to 70 pounds (18.1–31.7 kg) of dry food each month. They require extra-big clippers for their massive nails, a sleeping crate the size of a minivan, and monstrously huge toys to fit in their monstrously huge mouths. Mastiffs also dig, snore, and drool by the gallon. Owners often keep slobber rags to wipe off their dogs' mouths—and their walls and floors. These hulking canines can be problematic with cats and other small animals if not carefully trained at an early age. Also, be advised that the mighty mastiff, like all giant breeds, produces movements that would make Mozart proud. If you don't poop-scoop regularly, your backyard will turn into a Superfund site in short order. These dogs are also very sloppy eaters and drinkers. After visiting the water bowl, they will leave a trail of liquid through the house. They can knock over toddlers and old folks (and home furnishings) with one swipe of their massive tail.

DOG TRAITS

WHO SHOULD GET THIS DOG?

An individual or family with the cash necessary to support it in style and the inclination to give it the love and attention it craves. This is an enormous dog that will take up a lot of time and a lot of space.

OWNER TRAITS

Special Perks: A stern voice is all a competent owner needs to control a well-trained, socialized mastiff. These dogs require regular walks and fun frolics, but nothing excessive. The typical mastiff prefers stretching out across your bed or crashing on the couch, so you may have to coax it out the door.

Bugs in the System: Mastiffs can face a raft of genetic difficulties, including hip and elbow dysplasia, heart disease, immune disorders, and eye problems.

If someone broke into my house, this dog would: Stand still and stare. This alone should ward off most intruders. If not, the mastiff will release a powerful, savage-sounding bark. And if that doesn't work, they'll kick butt. The whole process takes about five seconds. Mastiffs act and look lethargic, but when necessary they can move like lightning.

If you like the mastiff, check out: The more streamlined (and less drool-intensive) Great Dane. Or the slightly smaller bullmastiff.

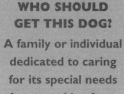

Weight: *20–31 pounds (9–14 kg).* **Height:** *16–23 inches (40.6– 58.4 cm).* **Build:** *Slim and graceful.* **Coat:** *None, save for a tuft on the head and a few hairs on the tail.* **Brains:** *Responds well to training.* **Bladder Matters:** *No special house-training issues.*

The Incredible Origin: The origins of this bizarre-looking breed are hazy, to say the least. Sometimes called the Xoloitzcuintli in its native Mexico, it is said to have been revered by the Aztecs as the earthly repre-sentative of the underworld god Xolotl. But while the Aztecs found the hairless to be divine, other tribes found it merely delicious. That is, delicious to *eat.* Today the hairless is enjoyed as a house pet rather than an entrée. It is available in three sizes: standard, miniature, and toy. About a third of all puppies in hairless litters are born with coats of fine hair. These are called powder puffs.

Trademark Traits: The typical hairless is reserved with strangers, open and loving with its family, and good with chil-dren, as long as they are gentle and respectful. This dog can be extremely sensitive—so sensitive that it should never be addressed in harsh tones. Its skin is as soft as a baby's butt. Legend once held that sleeping with this dog could "draw off" malaria and other diseases.

Headaches and Hassles: There's no way to say this diplomatically. To some people, the hairless looks and feels *creepy.* Also, one can never forget that the lack of a coat leaves this dog naked to the elements. It needs warm clothing (and moisturizer) in winter, and in summer can't go outdoors for any length of time without sun-screen.

Special Perks: No fleas, no shedding, very few allergy concerns. A well-socialized hairless gets along well with other dogs and even cats. Because it lacks a layer of insulating hair to hold in body heat, the skin of the hairless feels peculiarly warm. This (along with its near-overwhelming desire to always be close to its owner) makes it an ideal bed warmer on cold nights.

M	🛡	🐾

DOG TRAITS

WHO SHOULD GET THIS DOG?

A family or individual dedicated to caring for its special needs for everything from ample love and warmth to ample skin care. This is not a good choice for fami-lies with very young children, or for some-one looking for a walking companion. It would, however, do well in an apartment.

OWNER TRAITS

Bugs in the System: This dog requires more skin care than an aging Hollywood actress. It is susceptible to skin irritation, sunburn in summer, and normal wear and tear. Also, stock up on sweaters for winter. Eye and dental problems are common concerns. This dog can, unlike many canines, sweat through its skin.

If someone broke into my house, this dog would: Raise the alarm with a hail of barks. Quirky appearance aside, the hairless is a pretty good watchdog. And who knows, perhaps the intruder will be so freaked out by the sight of your hairless dog that he'll bolt.

If you like the Mexican hairless, check out: Another tiny dog with almost no hair, the Chinese crested.

Miniature Pinscher

Weight: 8–10 *pounds (3.6–4.5 kg).* **Height:** 10–12 *inches (25.4–30.5 cm).* **Build:** *Small and dainty.* **Coat:** *Very short hair, in colors ranging from black and tan to solid tan.* **Brains:** *Very intelligent, but hard to train. If you yell at a "min pin," it'll shut down.* **Bladder Matters:** *No particular house-training problems.*

The Incredible Origin: This miniscule breed was developed in Germany to hunt rats. The tan version looks somewhat like a Chihuahua, and the black and tan looks like a Doberman pinscher "Mini-Me."

Trademark Traits: The personality of the min pin is very similar to that of a terrier—tough, energetic, combative. It is utterly devoted to its family but won't be content to sit on a silk pillow all day. Don't pander to this dog or you may find yourself the subject of a foot-tall tyrant.

Headaches and Hassles: Not good with very small children. Handle a min pin roughly and you're asking to be bitten. It's also a peerless escape artist, using its lightning speed and superb jumping ability to dart out doors and leap fences. For this reason it must always be leashed in public. Miniature pinschers also like to steal and eat items such as pencils, paper, and small toys.

Special Perks: The min pin has an incredibly endearing personality and is always ready for energetic play. Exercise needs are minimal (a stroll down the street, a tear through the living room), and its short coat is effortless to maintain. A "bath" can consist of a washcloth wipe-down.

Bugs in the System: Miniature pinschers are generally healthy, but they can suffer from joint problems and various eye issues. Pregnant females need close medical supervision. Finally, the min pin's natural ears are floppy. If you want them pointed, it must be done surgically.

If someone broke into my house, this dog would: Sound the alarm. The min pin, suspicious of strangers and prone to bark at outside disturbances, makes a very good watchdog for its size.

If you like the miniature pinscher, check out: The Chihuahua, which is startlingly similar to the min pin.

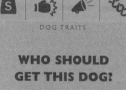

DOG TRAITS

WHO SHOULD GET THIS DOG?

Because of its neat habits and modest demands for exercise, the min pin can make an excellent apartment dog (provided its penchant for barking is controlled). If it gets lonely, the standard solution is to purchase a second one. Trust us, you've got room.

OWNER TRAITS

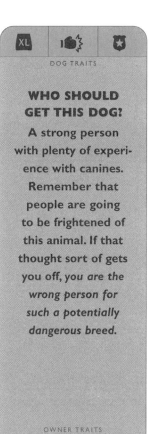

Weight: 110–154 pounds (49.5–69.3 kg). **Height:** 23–29 inches (58.4–73.7 cm). **Build:** Massive, heavily muscled body. **Coat:** Short coat in colors ranging from black to brindle to fawn. **Brains:** This breed has the intelligence to learn, but often lacks the desire. The terms "stubborn," "lazy," and "independent" have been used to describe the Neo's attitude toward obedience classes. **Bladder Matters:** No special house-training problems.

The Incredible Origin: Canines similar to the "Neo" were used as fighting and war dogs as far back as the Bronze Age. Allegedly a descendant of the giant dogs used as combatants in Rome's Colosseum, today's model was saved from extinction after World War II by a handful of breeders.

Trademark Traits: If the devil was a dog, he'd look like a Neo. This breed hasn't forgotten its bloody heritage. It is suspicious of strangers, aggressive toward other dogs (particularly those of the same sex), possessive of its owner and home, and able to inflict appalling damage in a heartbeat. These dogs must be carefully socialized from puppyhood. The owner's dominance must be constantly reinforced, though not by physical punishment—a foolhardy practice with such a massive specimen.

Headaches and Hassles: Neapolitan mastiffs drool and are very sloppy eaters. It's wise, if possible, to have them take meals outdoors. However, they aren't outdoor dogs. Most importantly, they can die from heatstroke. They crave the companionship of their family, and if denied it, they can suffer separation anxiety.

Special Perks: A Neo, if given proper training and socialization, is a friend and guardian without peer.

Bugs in the System: They can suffer from bloat, bone cancer, cardiac difficulties, eye problems, and orthopedic afflictions.

If someone broke into my house, this dog would: Be virtually unstoppable. Nothing enrages a Neo quite like a perceived threat to its family.

If you like the Neapolitan mastiff, check out: The bullmastiff, which is about the same size as the Neo but *slightly* less scary.

DOG TRAITS

WHO SHOULD GET THIS DOG?

A strong person with plenty of experience with canines. Remember that people are going to be frightened of this animal. If that thought sort of gets you off, *you are the wrong person for such a potentially dangerous breed.*

OWNER TRAITS

Newfoundland

Weight: 100–180 pounds (45–81 kg). ***Height:*** 25–29 inches (63.5–73.7 cm). ***Build:*** Very large and powerful. ***Coat:*** Very heavy, double coat in black, brown, and black and white. ***Brains:*** Eager to learn, and capable of mastering very complex training. ***Bladder Matters:*** No special house-training problems.

The Incredible Origin: This mighty dog likely arose in the Newfoundland region of Canada, the product of matings between various working breeds. The happy result is a gentle giant that's as useful as it is powerful. Over the centuries "Newfies" have helped fishermen pull in their nets, been used as draft animals, rescued sailors from shipwrecks, and have served as protectors of children. It's such a great dog that the poet Lord Byron actually singled it out for praise.

Trademark Traits: A well-bred Newfie is laid-back and utterly steady. They will tolerate the attention of children long after most other dogs would either walk away or nip someone. And due to their genetic background, they also love water. They even have webbed toes. Take your Newfie swimming and it will be eternally grateful. And don't worry too much about how to dry it. Water rolls off their coats like raindrops off a newly waxed car.

Headaches and Hassles: When this dog sits around the house, it sits *around* the house. Don't underestimate how much real estate a Newfie can take up. These dogs drool in thick ropes, and their spittle has the consistency of library paste. This breed needs a daily combing, and at least once a year it "blows" its prodigious coat, shedding enough hair to fill several grocery sacks. It would be unwise to purchase clothing or furnishings that clash with black hair.

Special Perks: Loyalty and gentleness, thy name is Newfoundland. A well-trained, well-bred Newfie will take an almost maternal interest in you and yours. This is the kind of dog that can (and has) rescued families from fires and other potential calamities. And should the need ever arise, this dog is capable of rescuing a

---

DOG TRAITS

WHO SHOULD GET THIS DOG?

A family or individual that's willing to make room, both literally and metaphorically, for a lifelong companion. Always remember that Newfies are utterly devoted to their families. Being given up for adoption can devastate these loyal, loving creatures.

OWNER TRAITS

drowning man and hauling him back to shore. If you're willing to commit to a plus-size canine relationship, this is one dog that won't let you down. It also, in most cases, gets along well with cats and other dogs.

Bugs in the System: Hip dysplasia can be a big issue. Bloat and diseases of the heart are other worries. This is an absolutely terrible dog for people who live in warm climates. Their life span is comparatively short—about 10 years.

If someone broke into my house, this dog would: Scare him off with his tremendous size. The Newfie isn't famous for its guarding ability, but usually the mere sight of this enormous black dog is enough to send the average trespasser packing. And if push comes to shove, even this laid-back breed will protect its family.

If you like the Newfoundland, check out: The snow-white Great Pyrenees, which looks like a Newfoundland that fell in a vat of bleach.

*Weight: 10–13 pounds (4.5–5.9 kg). **Height:** 9–12 inches (22.9–30.5 cm). **Build:** Sturdy, with short legs. **Coat:** Coarse hair, in shades ranging from red to tan to grizzle. **Brains:** Intelligent, but sometimes willful. However, both breeds want to please their owners and will learn if properly taught. **Bladder Matters:** No special house-training problems.*

The Incredible Origin: The Norfolk and Norwich are basically the same dog. The only difference is that the Norwich has pointy ears, while the Norfolk has floppy ears. Because the owners of floppy-eared models complained that the pointy-eared dogs won all the competitions, in 1964 they were divided into two distinct "breeds." The Norfolk/Norwich was originally developed to chase, corner, and harass small game. Joan Rivers (who was originally developed to chase, corner, and harass *celebrities*) owns two Norwiches, plus a Boston terrier.

Trademark Traits: Like many small terriers, these breeds were born to fight—and it shows. Though they display unreserved affection for their families and seem to enjoy children, they can be combative toward strangers, both human and animal. They are also slightly full of themselves, and may lord it over a weak owner.

Headaches and Hassles: These dogs love to dig, and they can create horrific excavation sites if left unsupervised. They may also become "recreational barkers." They will attack unfamiliar dogs and bolt after squirrels and other small animals. For this reason they must always be leashed in public. They can get along with cats, but usually only if socialized to them during puppyhood.

Special Perks: These dogs make excellent companions. Their coats require regular brushing but otherwise are easy to maintain. If properly introduced, they can get along with other dogs.

Bugs in the System: Though in general very hardy, these dogs can sometimes suffer from back problems and skin disorders.

If someone broke into my house, this dog would: Bark furiously and relentlessly.

If you like the Norfolk and Norwich terriers, check out: The cairn terrier, a close relative of these breeds.

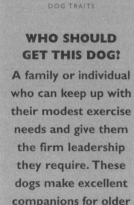

DOG TRAITS

WHO SHOULD GET THIS DOG?

A family or individual who can keep up with their modest exercise needs and give them the firm leadership they require. These dogs make excellent companions for older people—older people who don't coddle them too much. Apartment life can also work, provided they get outdoor time.

OWNER TRAITS

*Weight: 60–110 pounds (27–49.5 kg). **Height:** 20–24 inches (50.8–61 cm). **Build:** Sturdy and muscular. **Coat:** Coarse, long hair in gray, blue, and other colors, usually with white markings. **Brains:** Very intelligent and capable of learning complex behaviors. **Bladder Matters:** No special house-training issues.*

The Incredible Origin: Developed in England for herding cattle and sheep, it was (and still is) sometimes called the bobtail, because its tail was usually docked.

Trademark Traits: The big, fluffy sheepdog looks like an amiable puffball, but under all that hair is a smart, burly herding dog. The typical sheepdog needs lots of exercise and can be combative with other canines. It will also be utterly devoted to you and yours.

Headaches and Hassles: If you keep your sheepdog's coat long, get used to doing a lot of combing. Without several grooming sessions each week, all that long fur will quickly turn into a matted mess of dreadlocks. In summer, some owners simply do away with the hassle by giving their pooches very short, very unsheepdoglike, utility haircuts. These dogs require a steady fitness regimen, lest they apply their energy to tearing up the yard and/or house. Just don't exercise them excessively in hot weather. And be forewarned, some sheepdogs drool so profusely that their spit-soaked chin hair turns yellow.

Special Perks: You have to comb these dogs a lot, but at least they don't shed all that much. And what they do shed is very obvious and easy to vacuum away.

Bugs in the System: Hip dysplasia is a big issue, along with various eye problems and thyroid disorders. The ears require regular cleaning. Also, sheepdogs can put on weight. You may not notice because their ample coats conceal it better than a baggy shirt.

If someone broke into my house, this dog would: Some might put up a fight, some (most) might not. However, most will bark, and their deep bark sounds very intimidating—even if the average sheepdog won't back it up.

If you like the Old English sheepdog, check out: The bearded collie, which looks like a half-scale Old English.

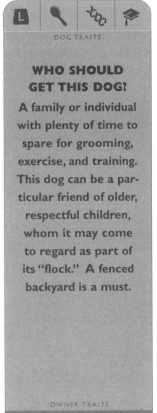

DOG TRAITS

WHO SHOULD GET THIS DOG?

A family or individual with plenty of time to spare for grooming, exercise, and training. This dog can be a particular friend of older, respectful children, whom it may come to regard as part of its "flock." A fenced backyard is a must.

OWNER TRAITS

*Weight: 7–10 pounds (3.2–4.5 kg). **Height:** 8–11 inches (20.3–27.9 cm). **Build:** Fragile. **Coat:** Long, silky white hair with patches of any color. **Brains:** Smart and eager to please. **Bladder Matters:** Can be difficult to house-train.*

The Incredible Origin: Versions of this lively little dog have been trotting around Europe for centuries. Actually, "trotting" is probably the wrong word. The papillon's traditional habitat was in the lap of a doting, upper-crust mistress. Marie Antoinette is said to have walked to the guillotine with one in her arms. Today it is rapidly gaining popularity as the Chihuahua's only serious rival in the category of Dogs So Small They Can Be Mistaken for Squirrels.

Trademark Traits: Referring to the pint-size pooch's ample ears, papillon means "butterfly." It was bred to be an entertaining companion, and it fulfills that function admirably. Papillons are utterly devoted to their masters, love to cuddle, and have beautiful, expressive faces. They're also not above roughhousing on the family-room floor.

Headaches and Hassles: Papillons can become obsessive barkers.

Special Perks: A well-behaved papillon is a great apartment dog. Its exercise needs are minimal, it eats like a bird, and its naturally clean habits make maintenance a breeze. About all one has to do is pay attention to it (a papillon won't tolerate being ignored) and regularly comb its silky hair.

Bugs in the System: The papillon is a healthy dog, though it does occasionally have knee and eye problems. It can also be sensitive to common anesthetics.

If someone broke into my house, this dog would: Like a slightly too sensitive home security system, a papillon will sound the alarm at the approach of any stranger.

If you like the papillon, check out: The Chihuahua and Pomeranian, both of which are roughly the same size as the papillon, but with far more attitude.

DOG TRAITS

WHO SHOULD GET THIS DOG?

This dog is ideal for homeowners, apartment dwellers, singles, families, and retirees. About the only people it's not good for are small children. Unfortunately, this breed isn't easy to obtain. Puppies are rare (litters may consist of only one or two), so responsible breeders treat them like treasure.

OWNER TRAITS

Pekingese

Weight: 8–10 pounds (3.6–4.5 kg), though some individuals fall far above this range. **Height:** 6–9 inches (15.2–22.9 cm). **Build:** A big head and a stocky, barrel-shaped body carried about on very short legs. **Coat:** Long, long hair, in pretty much every color known to humanity. **Brains:** Definitely not the brightest breed at the bark park. **Bladder Matters:** It takes a while for Pekes to get the hang of peeing outside.

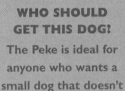

The Incredible Origin: The Pekingese has perched on couches, looking haughty, for hundreds (perhaps thousands) of years. Developed in China, it was a pampered ornament of the emperor's court. Particularly small ones were kept in the sleeves of nobles' robes. It came to the West in 1860 when five were looted by British troops from the imperial summer palace. Those dogs were taken halfway around the world, then plopped back down into the laps of luxury. Two pairs were given to duchesses, and one, bearing the exquisitely un-PC name of Looty, was presented to Queen Victoria herself. From that little group (with later additions) came the Pekingese we know today.

Trademark Traits: The "Peke," though bred primarily to *look* interesting, also has a unique personality. Though smaller than a decorative toss pillow (and serving roughly the same function), it can be quite spunky if it chooses. It is so brave and self-assured it will even, if given half the chance, try to pick fights with other dogs and attempt to dominate its owner. They walk with an unusual, highly amusing rolling gait.

Headaches and Hassles: The Peke's crowning glory is its mass of long, glossy hair—hair with which you will become intimately familiar, because you will have to comb it several times a week (professional grooming is also required). Here's a dirty little secret: If maintenance proves too daunting, all that silky stuff can simply be trimmed away, leaving the dog with a crew cut of soft, downy fur. Purists may gasp, but the dog won't mind at all—especially during the hot summer months.

Special Perks: This Chinese breed has a very American attitude

DOG TRAITS

WHO SHOULD GET THIS DOG?

The Peke is ideal for anyone who wants a small dog that doesn't demand much in the way of exercise. Be advised, however, that it will still require training and plenty of loving attention. It's an excellent choice for retirees.

OWNER TRAITS

toward physical exertion—it detests it. Apartment dwellers and people with 9-to-5 jobs will be gratified to know that their Peke will not greet them at the door every evening with its leash in its mouth, whining to go out. Some despise marching around so much that they will simply lie down on the sidewalk and refuse to walk any farther, forcing you to carry them home. Although we can relate, you still need to inflict some regular exercise. Without it, Pekes can pack on weight faster than yo-yo dieters.

Bugs in the System: This breed can suffer from corneal ulcerations, pinched nostrils, and umbilical hernias, among other things. Their eyes can be quite fragile. Prolonged exertion in hot temperatures can cause heatstroke. The folds in the face must be regularly cleaned, to keep them free of gunk. Females often have difficult pregnancies, and should be closely monitored by a veterinarian.

If someone broke into my house, this dog would: Bark. Pekes love to bark. As a matter of fact, you need to be careful that they don't turn it into a hobby.

If you like Pekingese, check out: The Tibetan spaniel, which may be the fore-bear of the Pekingese. Or it may not. However, the two breeds look so similar that if they were human beings, someone would long ago have filed a paternity suit.

Weight: 3–7 pounds (1.4–3.2 kg). **Height:** 7–12 inches (17.8–30.5 cm). **Build:** Fine-boned. **Coat:** Extremely fluffy fur, in colors ranging from black to orange to cream. **Brains:** Very intelligent and trainable. **Bladder Matters:** No particular house-training problems.

The Incredible Origin: Back in the nineteenth century, when all sorts of toy dogs were in vogue, German breeders developed this miniaturized version of the spitz. Queen Victoria was a particular fan of this breed. The original Pomeranian weighed about 30 pounds (13.6 kg), but as its fame grew, its dimensions shrank. Today the only way they can look impressive is by standing next to the even-smaller Yorkshire terrier or Chihuahua.

Trademark Traits: The Pomeranian may be little, but it has plenty of big-dog attitude. They are possessive of their owners, distrustful of strangers, and can be combative with other dogs. That said, they are also lively, loving, and incredibly amusing. A tiny "Pom" dancing on its hind legs is almost too cute for words.

Headaches and Hassles: Pomeranians can be a bit skittish, and boy can they bark. Particularly incorrigible ones may bark to announce the arrival of a guest, continue barking hysterically the entire time said guest is on the premises, then keep barking even after the person has departed. The Pomeranian can be aggressive with other dogs—even dogs many times its size. For this reason it should always be kept leashed in public. The Pomeranian isn't good around small children, and it must be handled in a firm but loving way if you want it to listen to you. They also shed profusely, and can fill their home with fur when they "blow their coats," which they will do at least once a year. To keep things livable, the little dog should receive daily or almost-daily brushing sessions. Otherwise its coat will quickly become a tangled mess.

Special Perks: The Pomeranian makes a vivacious and spirited pet. It cherishes its owner, but is not clingy or overly needy. Its antics with toys are endlessly amusing. If carefully introduced, it gets along well with other dogs—and even cats.

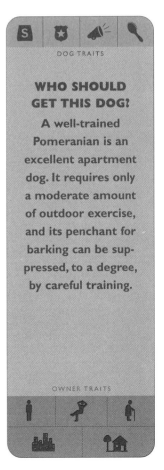

DOG TRAITS

WHO SHOULD GET THIS DOG?

A well-trained Pomeranian is an excellent apartment dog. It requires only a moderate amount of outdoor exercise, and its penchant for barking can be suppressed, to a degree, by careful training.

OWNER TRAITS

Bugs in the System: Subject to eye and knee problems. This breed has particular difficulties with its teeth, which are tartar magnets. They can lose a lot of them as they age.

If someone broke into my house, this dog would: Bark like crazy. Pomeranians are very good watchdogs for their size. They'll bark to alert you of an approaching stranger, and may even bark to announce said stranger's departure.

If you like the Pomeranian, check out: The equally mouthy and frenetic Yorkshire terrier. Or the engaging but more passive Papillon.

Weight: *45–70 pounds (20.3–31.5 kg).* **Height:** *15–24 inches (38.1–61 cm).* **Build:** *Slim but muscular.* **Coat:** *Dense, curly, wooly hair in solid colors ranging from black to brown to white.* **Brains:** *Arguably the smartest, most easily trained dog you will ever meet. It likes to learn, and it won't give you any guff during lessons. For generations they've been popular with circuses, because they're easy to educate and unflappable in front of crowds.* **Bladder Matters:** *No special house-training problems.*

The Incredible Origin: Versions of this curly-coated canine have been bounding around northern Europe for centuries. Today's model is, believe it or not, a sporting dog originally used to retrieve game from water. Those bizarre, bulbous-looking haircuts it sometimes sports were intended to make it a better field dog—or so the story goes—by keeping the leg joints, chest, and head warm, but freeing the hindquarters for efficient dog paddling. The poodle was an enormously popular companion dog during much of the twentieth century, leading to the development of a smaller miniature poodle and an even-smaller toy poodle. In keeping with their roots, these dogs love to get wet—be it in a swimming pool or mud puddle.

Trademark Traits: It's a shame this breed has such a wussy image, because it makes a great guy dog. If one can get past the froufrou haircuts (which most people don't bother with, anyway), you'll find a steady, loyal, highly intelligent former sporting dog that likes to goof around (particularly in water) when you do and likes to pile up in the Barcalounger when you do, too. Carefully bred poodles love people, tolerate children, and get along well with other animals, including cats.

Headaches and Hassles: If you're a guy and you adopt a standard poodle, prepare to have your manhood questioned. This will include everything from sly glances at the dog park to close male friends who say things such as, "Couldn't you find anything you liked in the *men's* department?"

DOG TRAITS

WHO SHOULD GET THIS DOG?

The standard poodle is a good dog for almost anyone, though a fenced yard would come in mighty handy. Also, remember that though this is a poodle, it is a *big* poodle—potentially as big as, say, a Golden retriever.

OWNER TRAITS

Special Perks: The poodle's coat doesn't shed. It needs regular professional grooming but is easy to manage if you opt for a simple utility cut instead of something more frilly. By the way, if you don't cut or groom the poodle's hair at all, it develops into long, Rastafarian-style dreadlocks. Unfortunately for Bob Marley fans, these dreads smell bad. Poodles can be very long-lived, often reaching 15 years or more.

Bugs in the System: Allergies, skin conditions, various eye disorders, hip dysplasia, and bloat.

If someone broke into my house, this dog would: Spot an intruder, raise the alarm, and possibly take aggressive action as a last resort. Here's a hint to all you criminals. If you land in jail because your crime was foiled by an attack poodle, *keep that information to yourself.*

If you like the standard poodle, check out: The smaller miniature poodle. Or, if you're a fan of strange hairstyles, investigate the dreadlocked puli.

Weight: 15–17 pounds (6.8–7.7 kg). Height: 11–15 inches (27.9–38.1 cm). Build: Exactly the same as that of the standard poodle, only smaller. Coat: Dense, curly, wooly hair in solid colors ranging from black to brown to white. Brains: You can train these dogs to do just about anything, short of starting your car in the morning. Bladder Matters: No special house-training issues.

The Incredible Origin: This breed was developed for people who wanted to own a poodle, but not, say, *70 pounds of poodle*. Basically a shrunken standard, it was created by breeding runts to runts, producing ever-more-runty puppies. The resulting dog retained the standard's smarts and personality, but in a smaller, apartment-friendly package. The combination has made the miniature one of America's favorite breeds.

Trademark Traits: Like their bigger cousins, miniatures are bright, even-tempered, happy, and loving. However, they can be a pinch more petulant than their plus-sized progenitor.

Headaches and Hassles: Hassles? What hassles? You have to walk them and feed them and pay attention to them, but if you consider those to be hassles, you're not cut out for a dog of any breed. About the only "bad" thing one can say about them is that they can be a little needy—even jealous.

Special Perks: These dogs don't shed, they love to give and receive affection, and they are so intelligent they can seem almost humanlike in their reactions and relationships.

Bugs in the System: Subject to heart disease, epilepsy, diabetes, allergies, and various eye problems.

If someone broke into my house, this dog would: Bark furiously until the intruder fled, clutching his bleeding ears.

If you like the miniature poodle, check out: The even-smaller toy poodle.

DOG TRAITS

WHO SHOULD GET THIS DOG?

The miniature is ideal for both homeowners and apartment dwellers, singles and families. All it needs is love and attention. It also does well with older children who know how to treat it.

OWNER TRAITS

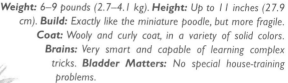

Weight: 6–9 pounds (2.7–4.1 kg). *Height:* Up to 11 inches (27.9 cm). *Build:* Exactly like the miniature poodle, but more fragile. *Coat:* Wooly and curly coat, in a variety of solid colors. *Brains:* Very smart and capable of learning complex tricks. *Bladder Matters:* No special house-training problems.

The Incredible Origin: Developed in the early twentieth century by people for whom the miniature poodle *just wasn't miniature enough*, this breed's natural habitat is a society lady's boudoir, or a tony high-rise apartment in midtown.

DOG TRAITS

WHO SHOULD GET THIS DOG?

A family (without very young children) or an individual looking for a pet who can serve as a confidant and four-legged psychiatrist. Don't be surprised if you find yourself talking to your toy poodle.

OWNER TRAITS

Trademark Traits: Devoted to its master (or, more often, mistress) almost to the point of jealousy. Can be somewhat nervous and combative around strangers, but is friendly and lively with those it knows.

Headaches and Hassles: The smaller the poodle gets, the twitchier it seems to become. While standard and even miniature poodles are famous for their lack of general aggression, some toys can be nippy.

Special Perks: Like their bigger cousins, the toy usually serves as a wonderful companion and worshipful sidekick. Its compact size makes it easy to transport, easy to exercise, and easy to care for.

Bugs in the System: The shrinking of the poodle from 70 to 7 pounds wasn't accomplished without cost. The breed's genetic defects include (but are not confined to) eye disorders, epilepsy, diabetes, and dislocated knees.

If someone broke into my house, this dog would: Bark in a most irritating and drawn-out manner.

If you like the toy poodle, check out: The Chihuahua, which is about the same size, but without the curly locks.

Weight: 14–20 pounds (6.3–9 kg). *Height:* 12–14 inches (30.5–35.6 cm). *Build:* Broad, stocky, square body and a great big head. *Coat:* Fine, short coat in silver, apricot, fawn, or black. *Brains:* Pugs aren't rocket scientists. However, they seem to harbor an innate desire to please their owners, which helps greatly as you try to impress bare-minimum concepts such as "come" into their canine brains. *Bladder Matters:* No special house-training issues.

The Incredible Origin: Nobody has a good grip on where the pug comes from, or even what its name means. Some say it's a European slang term for "dear one," while others contend it's a corruption of the Latin word *pugnus*, or fist. Though why someone would look at a snorting, bug-eyed pug and think "fist" is anyone's guess. As for its origin, some say it is a short-haired version of the Pekingese; others allege that it's some sort of miniature bulldog. What *is* known is that they aren't, and never were, working dogs. From day one, they were designed to do just one thing—trot around the house looking cute. A pug owned by the empress Josephine of France is said to have bitten her husband, Napoleon, when he tried to remove it from their bed.

Trademark Traits: The typical pug is a very atypical toy dog. Most toys can be somewhat skittish, but the pug is gregarious with both its family and strangers. Some even seem to like children, with whom they will romp and play.

Headaches and Hassles: Pugs snore. They also wheeze. And snort. It's like living with a sleep-apnea poster patient. Their facial wrinkles must be regularly cleaned, lest they fill up with gunk. And this breed also sheds enough for a dog twice its size.

Special Perks: Unlike many toy breeds, pugs aren't all that fragile. They groove on playing. And they seem to have less of that combative, Napoleon complex so common in some toys we could name (are you listening, Señor Chihuahua?).

Bugs in the System: Pugs are terribly vulnerable to temperature

DOG TRAITS

WHO SHOULD GET THIS DOG?
Someone who can provide the loving attention this breed thrives on. Also (very seriously), air-conditioning is a must. Retirees will find this breed to be a delightful companion. Just make sure you can tolerate the snoring.

OWNER TRAITS

extremes. In winter they can catch cold, and if taken out on hot days they can quickly overheat. *This is no exaggeration.* A pug can keel over and die after only 30 minutes of exertion in very hot weather. So keep them in the air-conditioning. They are also subject to allergies and breathing problems, and their eyes can be fragile. Make sure you don't overfeed, or they can become fat.

If someone broke into my house, this dog would: Raise the alarm loud and clear. Like many small dogs, the pug is a prodigious barker. *Unlike* many small dogs, it doesn't sound like a squeaky toy. If someone approaches, a pug will make the danger clear.

If you like the pug, check out: The Pekingese, its fun-loving, much hairier cousin. Or, perhaps, the larger French bulldog.

Weight: 20–35 pounds (9–15.8 kg). *Height:* 14–18 inches (35.6–45.7 cm). *Build:* Sturdy and muscular. *Coat:* A truly bizarre collection of usually-black dreadlocks. *Brains:* Highly intelligent and capable of learning the most complicated behaviors—if it feels like it. *Bladder Matters:* No special house-training problems.

The Incredible Origin: Now a hugely popular house pet in its native Hungary, this weird-looking animal once served as a sheepdog. Like just a handful of other canine herders, it would leap onto the backs of sheep to help push them along. Pulis are still famed leapers—as many an owner has discovered by, say, leaving a bologna sandwich unattended on a kitchen counter.

Trademark Traits: The puli is smart, lively, and not particularly interested in taking orders. This very independent breed loves its family and friends, but only a firm owner will be able to make it do what is expected. Pulis also aren't above manipulating the emotions of their humans to get what they desire. A puli will patrol its domain like a cop on the beat, investigating every sight and sound. It has keen eyesight—in spite of the fact that its eyes are barely visible under all that hair.

Headaches and Hassles: Pulis are very athletic and require a heavy dose of daily, vigorous exercise. If they don't get it, they may develop their own workout plan—destroying furnishings, excavating your landscape, and barking constantly. They will also chase and nip at moving objects, including joggers (bad), bikers (worse), and cars (worst of all). For this reason they must always be leashed in public. They will also pursue small animals, behave belligerently with dogs of the same sex, and will attack and kill cats. Not surprisingly, their coat requires a great deal of cleaning and maintenance. For instance, it takes about 24 hours for this dog to dry out from a bath. Pulis like to play rough, and they are therefore inappropriate for small children or the elderly. Poorly socialized ones will bark at every little thing, and their bark is particularly annoying.

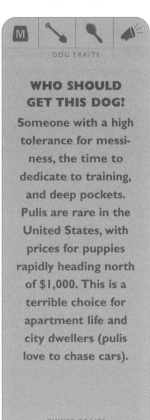

DOG TRAITS

WHO SHOULD GET THIS DOG?

Someone with a high tolerance for messiness, the time to dedicate to training, and deep pockets. Pulis are rare in the United States, with prices for puppies rapidly heading north of $1,000. This is a terrible choice for apartment life and city dwellers (pulis love to chase cars).

OWNER TRAITS

Special Perks: The puli's coat, which makes it look like the world's shortest Rastafarian, doesn't shed all that much. And there's no law that says your dog has to have dreadlocks. If you want, simply brush out its hair into a shaggy mane, or cut it short.

Bugs in the System: Suffers from hip dysplasia and various eye disorders. Pulis are also, for obvious reasons, not a great choice for persons living in places with warm climates.

If someone broke into my house, this dog would: Alert you to the danger. The puli is naturally suspicious of strangers and makes an excellent watchdog. Careful socialization and training is needed to make sure they don't become too aggressive toward unannounced or unexpected guests.

If you like the puli, check out: The komondor, which sports puli-like dreadlocks on a much larger body.

*Weight: 65–90 pounds (29.3–40.5 kg). **Height:** 24–27 inches (61–68.6 cm). **Build:** Powerful and sleek. **Coat:** Short, smooth, reddish-brown fur. **Brains:** These dogs are smart, but they will only pay attention to a dominant owner. **Bladder Matters:** No special house-training problems.*

The Incredible Origin: This unusual canine gets its name from the ridge of hair along its spine that runs in the opposite direction of the rest of its coat. It was developed in South Africa to hunt lions and other big game. A rarity just a few years ago, it has caught on in a big way in the United States.

Trademark Traits: The adult, well-socialized ridgeback can be pretty laid-back. But getting your ridgeback to be well-socialized can be a challenge.

Headaches and Hassles: Adults are usually quite calm and collected. But puppies (and by "puppies" we mean ridgebacks under the age of 2) are amazingly hyper. Without ample exercise and companionship, these dogs may turn destructive. Ridgebacks must be carefully socialized so that their natural aggressiveness and protectiveness doesn't get out of hand. These dogs love to chase prey, and they'll light out after just about any small, and not-so-small, game. They can be aggressive toward strange dogs and will attack cats. They also shed profusely, and their short hair is difficult to remove from upholstery and clothing. Ridgebacks also like to dig and will sometimes engage in "recreational barking."

Special Perks: Well-trained ridgebacks make handsome family pets and excellent guardians.

Bugs in the System: This is a healthy breed, though there are some issues with hip dysplasia and heart disorders. Ridgebacks can tolerate heat exceptionally well.

If someone broke into my house, this dog would: Are you kidding? Ridgebacks can route lions. They should have no trouble with the petty thieves in your neighborhood.

If you like the Rhodesian ridgeback, check out: The Great Dane, which was also originally bred as a powerful hunting dog.

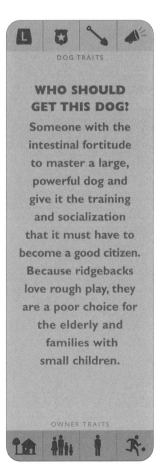

DOG TRAITS

WHO SHOULD GET THIS DOG?

Someone with the intestinal fortitude to master a large, powerful dog and give it the training and socialization that it must have to become a good citizen. Because ridgebacks love rough play, they are a poor choice for the elderly and families with small children.

OWNER TRAITS

Rottweiler

Weight: *85–130 pounds (38.3–58.5 kg).* **Height:** *22–27 inches (55.9–68.6 cm).* **Build:** *Sleek and muscular—like a Doberman pinscher on steroids.* **Coat:** *Very short hair, in black with rust-colored markings.* **Brains:** *Very intelligent and capable of learning pretty much anything a strong, experienced owner cares to teach it.* **Bladder Matters:** *No special house-training problems.*

The Incredible Origin: The breed takes its name from the German market town of Rottweil, around which it served, possibly for centuries, as a cattle herder. Cattle dealers stuck out in the middle of nowhere with large sums of cash came to appreciate this dog's intimidating strength—so much so that they fastened their purses around their Rottweilers' necks to keep the money safe. "Rotties" don't herd much anymore, but they have found other work as police dogs, guard dogs, and home companions. Its celebrity owners include Will Smith, who has two.

Trademark Traits: A well-bred Rottie is a rock, in every sense of the word. It seems well aware of its intimidating strength and looks, and in a low-level confrontation it often needs nothing more than a steady stare to make an opponent back down. Though laid-back among friends, it is very territorial and in many cases will defend its family and home savagely and to the death. So if you get one, make sure you tell your meter reader. Finally, Rottweilers possess a great deal of energy and like to work. If you don't have any cattle for yours to herd, then make sure it has other stimulating activities to engage it. Otherwise your Rottie can get bored—and a bored, restless dog of this size can be a real problem.

Headaches and Hassles: These strong dogs require a strong, steady hand. Training of a Rottie puppy must begin immediately and continue pretty much throughout the dog's life. Rotties will *definitely* make you prove your right to lead. However, never use corporal punishment on them. A Rottie may take only so much of this before it sends you to the emergency room. These dogs can

DOG TRAITS

WHO SHOULD GET THIS DOG?

A strong-willed, experienced dog owner with the energy to provide this canine with plenty of exercise, thorough training, and, most important of all, a loving home. Remember, all that's necessary to turn the average Rottweiler into an unmanageable dog is to chain it up in your yard and ignore it.

OWNER TRAITS

be combative with other canines, so always keep them leashed in public. They will also pack on weight if given the chance.

Special Perks: A well-trained, well-socialized Rottie is a fearless, devoted guardian of children—children above the age of 8, who know how to respect the animal. It also delivers the usual suite of dog-related goodies (including total loyalty) in spades. Its short, tight coat is a breeze to care for.

Bugs in the System: Some Rottweilers can suffer from various eye problems and from hip and elbow dysplasia.

If someone broke into my house, this dog would: Greet him ferociously. If you awaken in the middle of the night to cries of "OhGodHelpMe NOOOOOO!!" emanating from your living room, it means your Rottie is entertaining an uninvited guest. You might want to call the dog off while there's still something left for the police to arrest.

If you like the Rottweiler, check out: That other popular German import, the Doberman pinscher. Both provide excellent home defense.

Weight: 110–180 pounds (49.5–81 kg). Height: 25–27 inches (63.5–68.6 cm). Build: Stocky and powerful. Coat: Available in short and long coats. Brains: Average intelligence, though they can be slow to learn. Bladder Matters: No special house-training problems.

The Incredible Origin: Named after Saint Bernard de Menthon, who established a mountain-rescue station in the Swiss Alps around A.D. 1000, this huge breed was developed by the monks who ran the facility. The dog has been tinkered with numerous times, incorporating the blood of Newfoundlands, mastiffs, bloodhounds, and many other breeds to make the creature we know today. Contrary to popular belief, these dogs never carried casks of brandy around their necks.

Trademark Traits: The sad, jowly face of the Saint Bernard makes it look like the very picture of benevolence. If only that were the case. Beneath the cartoonish exterior is a powerful, willful dog that should only be handled by a strong, consistent owner. Training must start early, while the dog is still young and can be physically controlled. If you want it to be a good citizen, it should be socialized during puppyhood to dogs, cats, and other people.

Headaches and Hassles: A big Saint Bernard can pound down several heaping bowls of food each day. The breed also sheds excessively, especially in spring and fall. Its drooling will try the patience of a saint, as will its endless, infernal snoring. This dog can galumph through the house with all the grace of a fat, drunk fraternity brother in the midst of a pledge-week bender. So secure fragile bric-a-brac and consider rearranging your furniture to allow for its wide girth. Because this big dog can be like a furry, runaway train, it's an inappropriate breed for the elderly or homes with small children. Also, if Saint Bernards are left alone too long and become bored, they may start chewing things. Expensive things.

Special Perks: Once they are past their rambunctious youth, Saint Bernards settle down into quiet (when they're not snoring),

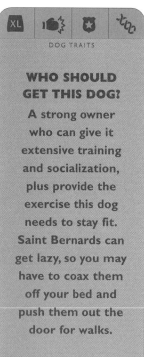

DOG TRAITS

WHO SHOULD GET THIS DOG?

A strong owner who can give it extensive training and socialization, plus provide the exercise this dog needs to stay fit. Saint Bernards can get lazy, so you may have to coax them off your bed and push them out the door for walks.

OWNER TRAITS

steady pets. This dog is a particular delight to watch as it romps through the snow on cold winter days. They can also be trained to pull carts and sleds.

Bugs in the System: The Saint Bernard has numerous health issues, including hip and shoulder problems, cancer, heart disorders, bloat, epilepsy, and eyelids that don't close properly. Obviously, this isn't a good choice for anyone living in an area with a warm climate. Though this dog needs regular exercise, it doesn't particularly seem to enjoy it. You'll need to pry it off the couch regularly and take it for walks.

If someone broke into my house, this dog would: Greet him with a bark that sounds like it comes from the ninth circle of Hell. If the dog actually gets hold of him, the intruder stands a pretty good chance of seeing that particular neighborhood personally.

If you like the Saint Bernard, check out: The Great Pyrenees, which made its living guarding herds while the Saint Bernard was digging out avalanche victims. Or the equally huge Newfoundland, which specialized in helping people who were drowning.

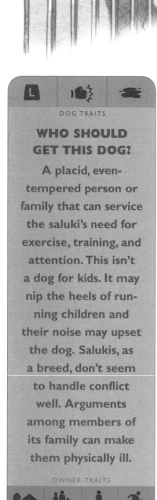

Weight: *31–55 pounds (14–24.8 kg).* **Height:** *23–28 inches (58.5–71.1 cm).* **Build:** *Sleek and muscular.* **Coat:** *Smooth and soft hair, in colors and color combinations ranging from white to red to black.* **Brains:** *Less than satisfactory. Training can be a long, frustrating process.* **Bladder Matters:** *Can be slow to house-train.*

The Incredible Origin: This classic Arabian hunting dog was traditionally used in tandem with a falcon. The falcon would spot and frighten prey (often gazelles) into the open, and the super-fast saluki would do the rest. Though fans allege it has paced the burning sands of Arabia for thousands of years, it didn't become popular in the West until the early twentieth century.

Trademark Traits: When it isn't hunting or exercising, the saluki can be surprisingly laid-back. It loves its family, but not to excess. And while it can run at speeds exceeding 40 mph (64.4 kph) when the situation demands it, when the situation doesn't, it's content to lounge for hours on the couch. Like many hounds, this dog is an independent thinker and can be easily distracted. Training will *not* go swimmingly. Even older dogs will "forget" their lessons if they get excited.

Headaches and Hassles: Salukis tend to be standoffish under the best of circumstances. If they aren't carefully socialized as puppies, this can harden into unpleasant suspiciousness. They are also tremendously fast, very independent, and prone to light out after any fast-moving object they see, be it a rabbit, bike, or car. For this reason they must always be leashed in public. The breed also requires lots of exercise, including long walks and chances to run at full speed in spacious fenced areas. Salukis are extremely athletic and can easily leap supposedly dog-proof fences. They can be dangerous to cats and even to small dogs. Puppies can be destructive. Adults aren't big on cuddling. And perhaps most unnerving of all, their silky-haired ears and close-cropped scalps give them a peculiar resemblance to the watermelon-smashing comedian Gallagher.

L

DOG TRAITS

WHO SHOULD GET THIS DOG?

A placid, even-tempered person or family that can service the saluki's need for exercise, training, and attention. This isn't a dog for kids. It may nip the heels of running children and their noise may upset the dog. Salukis, as a breed, don't seem to handle conflict well. Arguments among members of its family can make them physically ill.

OWNER TRAITS

Special Perks: The saluki's coat doesn't shed much and is easy to care for. The breed makes an excellent jogging partner. It can run great distances and is extremely tolerant of heat. Once out of its exuberant puppyhood, a properly socialized saluki makes a placid indoor companion.

Bugs in the System: May suffer from cancers, hypothyroidism, cardiac disorders, and various eye diseases.

If someone broke into my house, this dog would: Stand and watch. Salukis aren't big barkers, and they are utterly useless as bodyguards.

If you like the Saluki, check out: The more laid-back, easier-to-obtain greyhound, or the elegant-looking borzoi.

Samoyed

Weight: *44–66 pounds (19.8–29.7 kg).* **Height:** *16–22 inches (40.6–55.9 cm).* **Build:** *Sturdy and muscular.* **Coat:** *White and thick double coat.* **Brains:** *Intelligent but stubborn.* **Bladder Matters:** *Can sometimes be difficult to house-train.*

The Incredible Origin: The Samoyed is named after the Siberian tribe that used it for everything from herding to pulling sleds. Brought to the West in the nineteenth century, it became a tireless virtuoso sled dog employed on numerous polar expeditions.

Trademark Traits: The typical Samoyed is independent, energetic, and capable of shifting for itself. These characteristics are vital on the tundra, but can be problematic in the suburbs.

Headaches and Hassles: The Samoyed needs substantial amounts of exercise. Bad weather won't get you out of this, because the colder it gets and the more it snows, the more this dog likes it. Samoyeds can become extremely rowdy when excited and are prone to chasing and nipping at kids, cars, and pretty much anything else that moves. It can be aggressive toward other dogs and may kill cats. During spring and fall it sheds its massive undercoat. It's also prone to barking and to property destruction (indoors they may bite through drywall; outside they dig humungous holes) when bored or not properly exercised.

Special Perks: It's a very handsome dog and is supremely devoted to its family.

Bugs in the System: Subject to hip dysplasia, diabetes, many eye disorders, hypothyroidism, skin conditions, and allergies. Not surprisingly, it does very poorly in warm climates. If the coat is not regularly combed and cleaned, it can develop a funky smell.

If someone broke into my house, this dog would: Probably disappoint you. In spite of its rough and tough façade, the Samoyed is quite friendly and gregarious. It may bark at an intruder, but don't count on it doing much more.

If you like the Samoyed, check out: Those other arctic stalwarts, the Alaskan malamute and Siberian husky.

DOG TRAITS

WHO SHOULD GET THIS DOG?

Someone who can devote a great deal of time to training, exercise, and socialization. This dog is unsuitable for apartments, and its exuberance makes it a very poor choice for the elderly or families with small children. Samoyeds may also try to dominate a weak owner.

OWNER TRAITS

Schipperke

Weight: 12–18 pounds (5.4–8.1 kg). **Height:** 10–13 inches (25.4–33 cm). **Build:** Stocky. **Coat:** Thick, rough, black hair. **Brains:** Very intelligent, though it can be obstinate about training. **Bladder Matters:** Can be tricky to house-train.

The Incredible Origin: Developed in Belgium, the schipperke (allegedly its name means "little boatman," or something similar, in Flemish) originally lived on canal barges. These days it's a landlubber, serving as a peppery little companion dog.

Trademark Traits: It's hard to believe this miniscule pup was once called "the incarnation of the devil." Or maybe it isn't. The schipperke is intelligent, confident, willful, protective, and a bit high-strung.

Headaches and Hassles: When schipperkes lose their coats (usually twice a year, in spring and fall), the shedding is simply beyond description. Prepare to collect bags of black hair, to carry lint rollers as if they were fashion accessories, and to temporarily convert your wardrobe to clothing no lighter than black or navy.

Special Perks: The schipperke needs exercise, but it's so small that it can get a good workout just scampering around an apartment. It is devoted to its family, loves children, and makes an excellent watchdog. Properly socialized members of this breed usually get along well with cats and other dogs.

Bugs in the System: A mixed bag of problems, including epilepsy, hip dysplasia, and eye diseases.

If someone broke into my house, this dog would: Think it is far more formidable than it actually is. This dog, not much bigger than the stuffed toys they give away at state-fair midways, will furiously bark to raise the alarm, then may attack without thought for its own safety.

If you like the schipperke, check out: The keeshond, another barge-guarding breed.

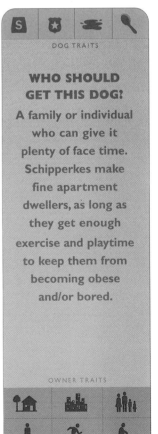

DOG TRAITS

WHO SHOULD GET THIS DOG?

A family or individual who can give it plenty of face time. Schipperkes make fine apartment dwellers, as long as they get enough exercise and playtime to keep them from becoming obese and/or bored.

OWNER TRAITS

*Weight: 30–50 pounds (13.5–22.5 kg). **Height:** 17–20 inches (43.2–50.8 cm). **Build:** Compact and muscular. **Coat:** Stiff and wiry coat. **Brains:** Very intelligent and amenable to all kinds of training—so long as it is treated fairly and not abused. A schnauzer's memory is excellent, especially when it comes to people who have wronged it. **Bladder Matters:** No special house-training problems.*

The Incredible Origin: This is the original stock from which the giant and miniature schnauzers were developed. The standard was created centuries ago in Germany, where it was used to hunt rats, protect property, and ride, Dalmatian-like, on carts and coaches.

Trademark Traits: All schnauzers display very terrier-like traits. They are highly possessive of their homes and families, belligerent toward other dogs and small animals, extremely intelligent and mischievous, and so strong willed that they can lord it over a weak-willed owner. They demand to take part in every aspect of family life, and they can make trouble if they feel slighted or ignored.

Headaches and Hassles: If you want your schnauzer to look like a schnauzer, be ready to shell out a small fortune for grooming.

Special Perks: The schnauzer's coat doesn't shed much. This breed is also a peerless home guardian and energetic playmate.

Bugs in the System: The standard is a healthy, long-lived breed. However, it can suffer from eye diseases such as progressive retinal atrophy and cataracts.

If someone broke into my house, this dog would: Announce the stranger's presence with a deep, intimidating bark that belies its size. If the situation escalates, this breed isn't above taking a couple of fingers off a burglar as a souvenir. The standard excels at watchdog work.

If you like the standard schnauzer, check out: The athletic, very territorial Airedale.

DOG TRAITS

WHO SHOULD GET THIS DOG?

A strong, energetic owner willing to provide the training this breed needs and the attention it craves. Early, careful socialization is essential for the high-spirited standard. This dog can be a great friend to children, but only if the kids are old enough to treat it with respect.

OWNER TRAITS

Weight: *55–80 pounds (24.8–36 kg).* **Height:** *23–28 inches (58.4–71.1 cm).* **Build:** *Solid and muscular.* **Coat:** *Thick, wiry coat, usually in black or salt-and-pepper.* **Brains:** *Very smart and capable of learning the most complex behaviors.* **Bladder Matters:** *No special house-training problems.*

The Incredible Origin: The giant is basically a standard schnauzer that's been bulked up by interbreeding with bigger, more powerful dogs. The resulting canine served as everything from a cattle driver to beer-hall bouncer. Though this is undeniably a strong, serious dog, there's something amusing about seeing that mustached schnauzer face on such a hulking frame. Today it's an increasingly popular house pet—which may or may not be a good thing, considering its strength and vigor.

Trademark Traits: Giants get along great with their family. It's the rest of the human race that bothers them. Highly protective and suspicious, they must be socialized from puppyhood to keep them from becoming paranoid or overly aggressive. They tend to "shadow" their owners, always remaining close and watchful.

Headaches and Hassles: This dog requires lots of exercise, and it can become hyper and destructive if it doesn't receive it. This breed can be skittish, so be sure to socialize them as puppies. They can be too rambunctious for very young children and too overprotective of older kids. In other words, if a playmate knocks your child down, and the giant schnauzer sees it, there could be trouble. Giants may fight with dogs of the same sex and try to chase and kill small animals—including cats. Finally, the schnauzer's perky little mustache and stylish haircut don't come naturally (or cheaply). In order to get them, you'll need to pay for regular professional grooming.

Special Perks: Well-bred, well-socialized giant schnauzers can be marvelous pets who show great devotion to their families. Also, they don't shed much and are a delight to train. All you need to do is make sure (in a nonviolent way, of course) that they understand who's boss.

DOG TRAITS

WHO SHOULD GET THIS DOG?

A strong-willed single, or a family with older kids. If given adequate training and leadership, a giant schnauzer makes a devoted pet and an excellent guardian of children. A big backyard (fenced, of course) comes in handy.

OWNER TRAITS

Bugs in the System: Can suffer from myriad eye problems, bone disease, hip dysplasia, joint problems, thyroid conditions, and more. Poorly socialized giants can actually become somewhat shy.

If someone broke into my house, this dog would: Be ready to rumble. All schnauzers are somewhat combative and protective of their domains, but the giant schnauzer has the physical substance to take that belligerence to the next level. This dog is leery of strangers but usually not paranoid. Once it sees the next-door neighbor a couple of times, it'll figure out she's not The Enemy. On the flip side, this dog may pick up on a stranger's bad vibes and suspicious behavior before you do.

If you like the giant schnauzer, check out: The Bouvier des Flandres, which sports a similar look and attitude.

*Weight: 10–18 pounds (4.5–8.1 kg). **Height:** 11–14 inches (27.9–35.6 cm). **Build:** Surprisingly muscular for such a small dog. **Coat:** Wiry and coarse coat. **Brains:** Very intelligent and easy to train. **Bladder Matters:** No special house-training problems.*

The Incredible Origin: Developed in nineteenth-century Germany, the miniature was a downsized version of the standard schnauzer that still made a good watchdog and rat hunter but was more appropriate as a household pet.

Trademark Traits: In America the miniature is classed as a terrier—not a bad idea, since it behaves so much like one. This breed is an experienced ratter, extremely protective of its family, aggressive toward other dogs (though it can get along with them if carefully introduced), and very energetic and intelligent.

Headaches and Hassles: Like other schnauzer types, the miniature costs a small fortune to groom. The breed is also very willful and will dominate a weak owner.

Special Perks: The miniature doesn't shed very much. It is a family dog without peer, sleeping with its owner and generally following its master wherever he or she goes.

Bugs in the System: Miniatures may suffer from skin disorders, bladder stones, liver disease, and cysts.

If someone broke into my house, this dog would: Bark its head off at the approach of strangers. Given its truculent attitude, it may even take on a trespasser.

If you like the miniature schnauzer, check out: The Border terrier, which can be just as territorial as the schnauzer, but doesn't require a fancy haircut.

DOG TRAITS

WHO SHOULD GET THIS DOG?

The miniature is an ideal dog for families and singles willing to service its robust need for attention and grooming. Because it is so small, a well-trained, well-socialized miniature can make a good apartment dog.

OWNER TRAITS

Weight: *66–106 pounds (29.7–47.7 kg).* **Height:** *28–32 inches (71.1–81.3 cm).* **Build:** *Muscular but graceful.* **Coat:** *Thick, shaggy, very dense hair in shades ranging from black to yellow to brindle.* **Brains:** *Can be somewhat stubborn about training and needs a firm hand.* **Bladder Matters:** *No special house-training problems.*

The Incredible Origin: This kissing cousin of the Irish wolfhound was used for centuries in Scotland to chase down deer. Guns eventually put this dog out of a job. Today it's mostly a companion animal.

Trademark Traits: The deerhound, like other fleet-footed sight hounds, is relatively reserved around the house. Although as puppies they can be extremely active, adults are content to pile up on the couch and camp out. Believe it or not, these huge dogs can become timid if not properly socialized.

Headaches and Hassles: This is a big dog that requires regular, vigorous exercise and a special, high-quality diet. Be advised that adult deerhounds won't hesitate to snatch food. It isn't much of a challenge, since their great height puts kitchen counters at eye level. Also, this breed can utter an alarming howl/whine when it feels upset or put out. Finally, because the deerhound will chase any small animal it happens to see, it be must be kept leashed in public at all times.

Special Perks: For a breed with such a long, very dense coat, the deerhound is relatively easy to groom. Though this dog is a powerful runner, if well exercised it will be content to just lounge around the house during its "off" hours. Deerhounds are legendary for their napping.

Bugs in the System: Like many large dogs, the deerhound suffers from a potentially long list of genetic troubles, including bloat, bone cancer, and heart disease. Interestingly, hip dysplasia often isn't a big issue. Be advised that while well-trained adult deerhounds are quite mannerly, puppies can be extremely boisterous, and they will test their owners' authority—and patience.

DOG TRAITS

WHO SHOULD GET THIS DOG?

An individual or family (preferably without very young kids) willing to invest the time and trouble necessary to make such a large dog feel loved and welcome. This is a very poor (indeed, nearly unworkable) choice for apartment dwellers and the elderly.

OWNER TRAITS

Common gambits may include attempting to commandeer the living room couch or, perhaps, your favorite chair. Like all young dogs, they will try to jump on people. You'll need to nip this in the bud, or one day face the spectacle of grandpa getting pancaked by your deerhound.

If someone broke into my house, this dog would: Protect your family. Unfortunately, they're of little use when it comes to property protection. If someone broke in while you were gone, they might not even bark. It just isn't their bag.

If you like the deerhound, check out: The even bigger Irish wolfhound, or the more elegant borzoi.

Weight: 18–23 pounds (8.1–10.4 kg). *Height:* 9–11 (22.9–27.9 cm). *Build:* Stocky, solid body with very short legs. *Coat:* Long, wiry outer coat in colors ranging from black to wheaten to numerous shades of brindle. *Brains:* Scotties are bright, but independent. They will accept basic training, but often won't sit still for the "roll over, play dead" routine. *Bladder Matters:* No special house-training problems

The Incredible Origin: Developed in the nineteenth century, this breed was also known as the "diehard"—which pretty much sums up its character. Set on short legs so it can chase game into its lair, the Scottish terrier possesses an oversized personality—along with an oversized set of teeth. It could be called the official lapdog of World War II. President Franklin Roosevelt had one. Eva Braun, Hitler's mistress, had two.

Trademark Traits: The Scottie's distinctive looks have for decades made it a trendy companion dog. That's too bad, because this bossy, diligent but reserved animal is nobody's fashion accessory. Scotties can be aloof with everyone but their family, to whom they give their unflinching loyalty. They must be carefully trained to channel their strong, dominant personalities into non-destructive pursuits.

Headaches and Hassles: Scotties *love* to dig, so don't leave one alone in your backyard unless you'd like it to install a root cellar. They also require professional grooming. Because this breed is quite active, it relishes regular walks. A sedentary Scottie is a bored Scottie. And a bored Scottie may amuse itself by taste-testing interior furnishings. Not surprisingly, they can be very aggressive toward other dogs. Finally, never allow a Scottie to go near deep water unsupervised. They swim about as well as bricks float. They cannot be trusted around small animals, and they must therefore be leashed at all times in public.

Special Perks: Well-trained, well-socialized Scotties make great companions and good friends for older, respectful children. When these same respectful children are in the throes of a sugar rush,

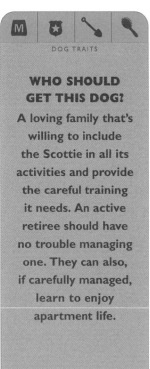

DOG TRAITS

WHO SHOULD GET THIS DOG?

A loving family that's willing to include the Scottie in all its activities and provide the careful training it needs. An active retiree should have no trouble managing one. They can also, if carefully managed, learn to enjoy apartment life.

OWNER TRAITS

Scotties will have the energy to keep up with them. They need to be near their families, but they won't constantly pine for affection. These dogs love a good game of fetch and smacking around squeaky toys.

Bugs in the System: This breed's short list of genetic problems includes a peculiar malady called Scottie cramp, which causes their muscles to suddenly lock up during exercise. Fortunately, bouts are usually short and cause no lasting damage. Other problems include a bleeding disorder called von Willebrand's disease, hyperthyroidism, and epilepsy.

If someone broke into my house, this dog would: Raise a ruckus. Scotties are highly territorial and celebrated barkers. And if push comes to shove, many won't hesitate to use their freaky big teeth to unzip an intruder from stem to sternum. Or, more accurately, from ankle to knee.

If you like the Scottish terrier, check out: The yin to the often all-black Scottie's yang, the West Highland white terrier.

Weight: 12–18 pounds (5.4–8.1 kg). **Height:** *12–15 inches (30.5–38.1 cm).* **Build:** *Trim, with a light frame.* **Coat:** *Long, silky hair almost identical to that of a collie. Color combinations include sable, tricolor, and blue merle.* **Brains:** *Apparently herding sheep takes a lot of smarts. Like most dogs formerly engaged in this line of work, the sheltie is extremely—almost disconcertingly—intelligent.* **Bladder Matters:** *No special house-training issues.*

The Incredible Origin: Though it looks like a miniaturized collie, this breed's origins are somewhat murky. Its forebears allegedly were herding dogs from the Shetland Islands off Scotland, but in more recent times it was crossed with various other breeds (including, probably, the collie) to refine its look.

DOG TRAITS

WHO SHOULD GET THIS DOG?

An excellent choice for active families with young (but not too young) children. You must be willing to give this dog plenty of attention and exercise. Otherwise it can go buggy from boredom, or use its ample intellect to cause mayhem. Active retirees may enjoy this breed.

OWNER TRAITS

Trademark Traits: A well-bred, carefully socialized sheltie makes an attractive, delightful companion. They bond strongly with their families and are easily trained. However, they can also be very high-strung. Remember how you felt the day you downed too many cups of coffee at work and couldn't sit still? That's how many shelties act all the time.

Headaches and Hassles: Shelties are one-person dogs—so much so that they may give their allegiance to only one family member, then act cool to everyone else. Some are so leery of strangers that they won't allow themselves to be touched by them. In public encounters it's not unusual for a sheltie to remain entirely fixated on its owner, even when another person is right in front of it, obviously trying to attract its attention. This sort of thing can get out of hand unless the dog is carefully socialized as a puppy. Their herding background has left them with a strong desire to chase things, including, unfortunately, cars. Some shelties also like to bark. And bark. And bark . . .

Special Perks: A well-bred sheltie is a joy to live with. While it's cool to strangers, it will never be cool toward you. They need regular exercise, which can be readily obtained in a moderately sized fenced yard. Its intelligence is another plus. But because it has so much on the ball, it will not be content to simply lounge around all day. It needs stimulating games and plenty of face time with its owners. Also, while all dogs are adept at reading human moods, the sheltie's skills border on clairvoyance. If you're inordinately mad, sad, or glad, this dog will know—perhaps before you do.

Bugs in the System: The coat needs regular brushing and professional grooming. Their shedding reaches near-Biblical proportions during spring and fall, when they lose their thick undercoats. Shelties are also given to eye problems, knee difficulties, and, occasionally, hyperthyroidism. They will overeat if given half a chance.

If someone broke into my house, this dog would: No one sneaks up on a sheltie. An intruder's arrival would be announced as soon as he crossed your property line.

If you like shelties, check out: The Border collie, a breed that's arguably even sharper than the sheltie, though somewhat less photogenic.

Shih Tzu

Weight: *9–16 pounds (4.1–7.2 kg).* **Height:** *10–11 inches (25.4–27.9 cm).* **Build:** *Sturdy and compact.* **Coat:** *Long, silky hair in a variety of colors.* **Brains:** *Easy to train.* **Bladder Matters:** *No special house-training problems.*

The Incredible Origin: In spite (or, more likely, because) of the fact that no one has a clue about the true origins of this Chinese lapdog, numerous improbable scenarios have arisen to fill in the historical blanks. Some say the breed was developed in the Byzantine Empire and sent to the Chinese emperor as a gift; others contend it was created by ancient mixings of the Tibetan Lhasa apso with the Pekingese. What's known for sure is that the Chinese guarded this dog so zealously that it wasn't introduced into the West until the mid-twentieth century. Today it's making up for lost time, lounging around exclusive apartments and elegant mansions the way it once strutted through the Forbidden City.

Trademark Traits: This pet of emperors makes a surprisingly lively little companion. It loves its owner and enjoys nothing better than being held, petted, and otherwise doted on. It's also not above a romp with a squeaky toy on the living room floor.

Headaches and Hassles: The Shih Tzu's long, flowing hair needs regular home brushing plus frequent professional grooming. Weekly baths are a good idea, as are daily face washings to keep the dog presentable and free of eye boogers. The long locks around its eyes are usually tied up and secured with a bow, which makes this dog look like a very hirsute member of a 1960s girls' singing group. It loves to eat and can pack on the poundage rather quickly.

Special Perks: If you don't want to hassle with this breed's hair, you can simply trim most of it away. Trust us, the dog won't mind. And once you take grooming off the table, the Shih Tzu's other demands can be pretty reasonable. This dog loves to be near its owner, but in most cases it will also easily tolerate spending the

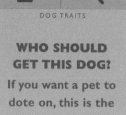

DOG TRAITS

WHO SHOULD GET THIS DOG?

If you want a pet to dote on, this is the dog for you. Shih Tzus are excellent for older people, singles, and families with older children. They're not good for families with young children, however, because these dogs cannot tolerate rough handling.

OWNER TRAITS

day alone while you're at work. Its bathroom needs are so modest that some people simply allow theirs to relieve themselves on newspaper. Others rig up cat litter boxes with a metal grid over the top, upon which the dog can stand to do its business. Exercise can be equally low-key, consisting of a short walk around the block and a few mad dashes through the house, during regular squeaky-toy fests.

Bugs in the System: Can suffer from ear infections and kidney problems. Their buggy eyes are vulnerable to injury and can become overly dry. Shih Tzus don't do well in warm weather, which can cause them to overheat.

If someone broke into my house, this dog would: Probably get stolen, right along with the silverware. Actually, that's not quite fair. The typical Shih Tzu will bark to announce a stranger—and then it will probably get stolen, right along with the silverware.

If you like the Shih Tzu, check out: The Shih Tzu's alleged ancestor, the Lhasa apso. Or its *other* alleged ancestor, the Pekingese. But no matter your choice, you're going to need a hairbrush.

Siberian Husky

Weight: *35–60 pounds (15.8–34.1 kg).* **Height:** *20–23 inches (50.8–58.4 cm).* **Build:** *Powerful and athletic.* **Coat:** *A thick double coat in a variety of colors and markings.* **Brains:** *Very intelligent, but hard to train—and to keep trained. Even a husky that's had an extensive education may not reliably come when called.* **Bladder Matters:** *No special house-training problems.*

DOG TRAITS

WHO SHOULD GET THIS DOG?

A strong individual or a family (without very small children) that can spend lots of time with it. The husky is a pack animal and wants to be with its family. Leave it alone all day, and you're asking to have your furnishings demolished.

OWNER TRAITS

The Incredible Origin: The Siberian husky was used in Siberia to pull sleds and herd reindeer. In the nineteenth century it was imported to North America, where it soon became the most celebrated of all sled dogs. For a while, this breed enjoyed almost Lassie-like fame, thanks to its participation in a 1925 dogsled relay that transported diphtheria serum over 600 miles of frozen tundra to the town of Nome, which was in the midst of a diphtheria epidemic. The dog team that handled the last leg of the trip was led by a Siberian named Balto, a statue of whom stands in Central Park in New York City. Nowadays, of course, the snowmobile has put this breed out of a job, but it still finds steady gigs as a cool-looking companion animal.

Trademark Traits: Though it resembles a wolf and has intimidating icy-blue eyes, the average husky is actually quite mellow. It's friendly with its family, friendly with strangers, by and large friendly with *everyone*. They're good with children, provided the children are good with *them*.

Headaches and Hassles: Ordinarily this dog's thick coat requires only routine brushing. But when it sheds in spring and fall, your furniture and floors can vanish under drifts of hair. It will waft onto your clothes, into your lungs, and onto your food. Get used to it. Huskies are incorrigible diggers, need vigorous exercise, and will attack, kill, and eat small animals (including cats). Also, they will run away if given half the chance. They require a fenced yard and must be leashed in public.

Special Perks: Huskies usually don't have problems with other dogs. Inherently docile, they will be content to cuddle up with you in the living room—after they've had their daily exercise, of course. For a big dog, they don't eat all that much. Huskies are, for obvious reasons, utterly impervious to cold. This does not mean, however, that they should be kept outside.

Bugs in the System: Because of their heavy coats, huskies don't do well in warm climates. When it's hot enough to turn on the air-conditioning, keep its outdoor activity to a minimum.

If someone broke into my house, this dog would: Welcome him with great enthusiasm. This breed, in spite of its scary appearance, is usually worthless for home defense.

If you like the Siberian husky, check out: Another burly sled dog, the Alaskan malamute. Or, if you'd like a burly, bristle-tailed guard dog, the Akita.

Spinone Italiano

*Weight: 62–82 pounds (27.9–36.9 kg). **Height:** 23–28 inches (58.4–71.1 cm). **Build:** Sturdy but somewhat slender. **Coat:** Rough, wirehaired coat in colors ranging from white to reddish-brown to white with orange. **Brains:** Intelligent and for the most part easy to train, though some possess a stubborn streak. **Bladder Matters:** No special house-training issues.*

The Incredible Origin: This bristly-looking dog is an Italian native, allegedly developed from French stock, and has been used for centuries as an excellent all-purpose hunting dog. It can track, point, and retrieve. It is also a strong swimmer.

Trademark Traits: The spinone is big enough to make a lot of trouble if it felt like it. Fortunately, it doesn't feel like it. Gentle and affectionate with its family, it can be somewhat reserved, even shy, around strangers. Spinones crave abundant affection and have no qualms about reminding their families of this. If you stop petting one before it wants you to stop, you may get a nose nudge or paw slap.

Headaches and Hassles: Spinones like to dig and to eat unauthorized finds, including dirt, sticks—even their own poop. Water, food, and dirt get trapped in its coarse beard, which often as not it cleans with a leisurely rub on the nearest wall or piece of furniture. When nervous or panting from exertion, it can drool (owners call this "spinone slime"). It will get rid of said drool by shaking its head vigorously, flinging the ropy saliva everywhere.

Special Perks: For a big dog, the spinone is uncommonly gentle. It loves its family, gets along with other animals (including cats), enjoys children, and is remarkably quiet around the house.

Bugs in the System: Although a very healthy breed in general, hip dysplasia is a concern. Also, you must clean its ears regularly.

If someone broke into my house, this dog would: Bark. Spinones possess a deep, intimidating bark, which they will employ whenever they spot a strange person or animal. However, when it comes to aggression, barking is about as far as they will go.

If you like the spinone, check out: The more reserved Weimaraner.

DOG TRAITS

WHO SHOULD GET THIS DOG?

An individual or family that can provide lots of training, exercise, and attention, and that doesn't mind cleaning up the occasional (or not-so-occasional) spinone-created mess. An ample fenced backyard is greatly appreciated.

OWNER TRAITS

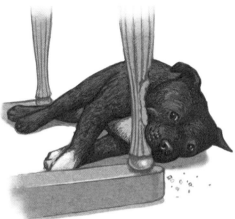

Weight: 23–38 pounds (10.4–17.1 kg). **Height:** 13–16 inches (33–40.6 cm). **Build:** Powerfully muscled, stocky body. **Coat:** Extremely short hair in colors and mixes ranging from red to brindle to black. **Brains:** Can be somewhat stubborn during training. **Bladder Matters:** No special house-training issues.

The Incredible Origin: A couple of centuries ago, "bull dogs" looked nothing like the big-headed, snuffling English bulldogs seen today. Back then they were actually expected to fight bulls and were therefore far more bloody-minded and athletic-looking. When bullbaiting and bearbaiting were outlawed in England, owners of these dangerous canines turned to dog fighting, producing even more agile four-legged gladiators by crossing bulldogs with terriers. Thus arose the Staffordshire bull terrier—a British "working man's dog" used for home defense and, in bygone days, the occasional organized fight. It was also kept fairly small, because your typical miner or tradesman couldn't spend a fortune on dog food. Today's version of the breed has mellowed out considerably and is, believe it or not, a popular companion animal. In England it is even nicknamed "The Nanny Dog" because it gets along so well with kids.

Trademark Traits: This granddad of the American stafforshire terrier (which is about twice its size) is dangerous to its enemies, real and perceived, but mellow and protective with its family. It seems particularly devoted to children (*its* children, not children in general). Though these dogs tend to tolerate lots of ear-pulling and poking from people they love, it is extremely important to *prevent* your kids from partaking of such behavior. This is a bad idea with any dog, but particularly with one that can bite through sheet metal.

Headaches and Hassles: All puppies like to nibble and gnaw, but make sure *these* puppies own a stock of tough-as-nails toys. Otherwise they'll use your Pottery Barn leather ottoman as a giant rawhide chew. Some of these dogs get along well with cats, but others most definitely don't. Adult Staffordshires have

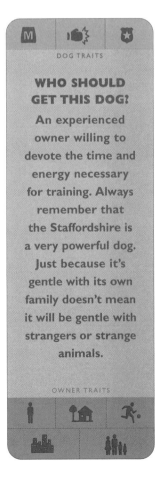

DOG TRAITS

WHO SHOULD GET THIS DOG?
An experienced owner willing to devote the time and energy necessary for training. Always remember that the Staffordshire is a very powerful dog. Just because it's gentle with its own family doesn't mean it will be gentle with strangers or strange animals.

OWNER TRAITS

problems with other canines, and they usually can't be trusted around them. They must *always* be leashed in public.

Special Perks: The coat is very low-maintenance. Staffordshires are very energetic, but regular walks and brief backyard skirmishes should suffice. Also, fans of guarding breeds can get all the intimidating cachet of one, but in a very small package. *However, wanting a scary-looking pet is a terrible reason to get this, or any, dog.*

Bugs in the System: Unlike some breeds, this dog doesn't have a mile-long list of genetic problems. However, it can suffer from cataracts and epilepsy, and it is prone to both heat exhaustion and (because of its extremely short coat) hypothermia.

If someone broke into my house, this dog would: Take him on. Staffordshires are small, but their jaws close with the force of a bear trap. And since they are devoted to their families, and are fearless and insensitive to pain, they won't hesitate to use those jaws in truly dangerous situations.

If you like the Staffordshire bull terrier, check out: Another great family friend, the English bulldog.

Weight: 9–15 pounds (4.1–6.8 kg). **Height:** 10–11 inches (25.4–27.9 cm). **Build:** Squat, short-legged. **Coat:** Long and flat coat, in any color or mix of colors. **Brains:** This dog is very easy to train but only through positive reinforcement. **Bladder Matters:** No special house-training problems.

The Incredible Origin: The Tibetan spaniel (which isn't really a spaniel) comes from Tibet, where it was allegedly used as a watchdog in Buddhist temples. It's called a "spaniel" to differentiate it from another breed, the Tibetan terrier (which isn't really a terrier).

Trademark Traits: The Tibetan loves its family but may be aloof with strangers. It's also very sensitive to its owner's changing moods.

Headaches and Hassles: Its barking can occasionally get out of hand. This little dog has a big mouth.

Special Perks: A great all-around lapdog. Its minimal exercise needs can be met with walks around the block and an occasional living room romp. And while the typical Tibetan will bark to announce strangers, the breed generally isn't "yippy."

Bugs in the System: Tibetans are very long-lived and not heir to very many hereditary illnesses. However, they can suffer from eye problems and allergies.

If someone broke into my house, this dog would: Go ballistic. These dogs may be small, but they are very effective watchdogs. If anyone so much as looks at your property in a strange way, the Tibetan will raise the alarm.

If you like the Tibetan spaniel, check out: A breed that's similar in looks and attitude, the Pekingese. Also, another famed guardian from the Himalayas, the Lhasa Apso.

DOG TRAITS

WHO SHOULD GET THIS DOG?

The Tibetan is good for young and old, families and singles. Be advised, however, that it isn't good with very young children. The breed is somewhat sensitive, and a few cuffs from a toddler are all that's needed to scar it emotionally for life.

OWNER TRAITS

*Weight: 48–66 pounds (21.6–29.7 kg). **Height:** 21–25 inches (53.3–63.5 cm). **Build:** Sleek, well-muscled frame. **Coat:** Short, rust-colored coat. **Brains:** Very intelligent but quirky and somewhat hard to train. **Bladder Matters:** No particular house-training problems.*

The Incredible Origin: The vizsla (a.k.a. the Hungarian pointer), like so many other breeds, gives us two origin stories to pick from—one that's more interesting but implausible and one that's not so interesting but *more* plausible. According to the first, the dog is one of the oldest of sporting breeds, developed hundreds of years ago by the Magyars (Hungarians). According to the other legend, it was produced relatively recently by crossing Weimaraners with various pointers (which isn't too hard to believe, since the two types look like clones to the untutored eye). Nevertheless, if you acquire one and people ask what it is, we recommend going with the Magyar story.

Trademark Traits: Vizslas are very "into" their owners. So much so that they are nicknamed "Velcro Dogs." They will watch you while you take a shower. They will watch you sleep. They will watch you relieve yourself, if you let them. Also, they like to carry things around—toys, one of your shoes, etc. You may also, at odd times, feel your vizsla carefully take your hand in its mouth. They will, in spite of their size, try to sit on your lap.

Headaches and Hassles: Vizslas need lots of training and exercise or they can become destructive. Puppies particularly so. These dogs can be a touch on the hyper side if they don't get their ya-yas out daily—and we're not talking about a walk around the block. Vizslas need regular excursions and an occasional off-the-leash run (in an enclosed, secure area, of course). Remember that these athletic dogs can clear fences 6 feet (183 cm) tall or higher. The vizsla is also an incorrigible gooser and crotch sniffer. They delight in jumping on people, will dig massive holes in your yard, and will steal food at any opportunity. They may also eat inappropriate things (pieces of their toys, etc.). They enjoy sleeping in high, comfy places. At best, you may find them on your couch. At

DOG TRAITS

WHO SHOULD GET THIS DOG?

A family or individual who can provide the dog the one-on-one, undying attention it requires—and can put up with its shenanigans. This dog will fit into an apartment—barely—but a home with a fenced yard is a better choice.

OWNER TRAITS

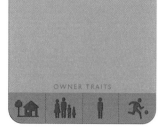

worst, you may come home from work to find your vizsla sprawled across the dining room table. Poorly socialized dogs can be timid.

Special Perks: In spite of everything, these dogs are very lovable. They are gentle with everyone and live for their families. Plus, careful training and regular exercise can go a long way toward curing most of their bad habits.

Bugs in the System: Vizslas are for the most part healthy and long-lived. However, some may suffer from hip dysplasia, hemophilia, and epilepsy, among other things. Some may develop food or skin allergies and be sensitive to common anesthestics.

If someone broke into my house, this dog would: Bark while the intruder crawls in through a window, then, its duty done, retire back to the sofa as said intruder cleans out the wall safe.

If you like the vizsla, check out: The slightly larger Weimaraner.

Weimaraner

Weight: 55–85 pounds (24.8–38.3 kg). *Height:* 23–27 inches (58.4–68.6 cm). *Build:* Trim, athletic, and muscular. *Coat:* Short coat, in varying shades of gray. *Brains:* Weims are generally quick learners. *Bladder Matters:* House-training can take awhile.

The Incredible Origin: Allegedly developed in the nineteenth century in Weimar, Germany, this hardy sporting dog did everything from retrieve birds to take on bears and wild pigs. Today, thanks primarily to William Wegman's wildly famous Weimaraner photos, it is an increasingly popular domestic pet. Which is not necessarily a good thing (see "Headaches and Hassles").

Trademark Traits: "Weims" (also known, by more than a few bemused owners, as "Weisenheimers") are very smart, but they are also startlingly independent thinkers who can sulk if they don't get their way. Managing them is like managing a human teenager—a teenager who can crash through the brush all day, looking for game. Training may present additional challenges. While they may master, without prompting, such feats as opening doors, unlatching gates, and even turning on faucets to get a drink, they may resist relatively simple lessons such as "sit," "stay," and, perhaps most of all, "come." Weims are also Houdini-like escape artists, able to tunnel under, leap over, or open the gates of, fences. A fired-up dog may also punch through a door or window screen like it wasn't even there. And they love to roll in stuff—the deader, the better.

Headaches and Hassles: These dogs cannot be ignored. If you ignore them, you're asking for everything from excessive barking to house-soiling to determined attacks on floors, furnishings, and walls. Weims must be well socialized to counter their tendencies toward shyness and/or aggressiveness. This dog may look mellow, but it requires a strong owner or it will take over the house. They shed copiously, dig up yards, drink sloppily, and their dander seems particularly irritating to some asthmatics. Also, they usually can't be trusted around cats or other small animals. They must always be leashed in public.

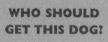

DOG TRAITS

WHO SHOULD GET THIS DOG?

Weims aren't a good fit for the elderly or for families with very small children. The dogs aren't usually aggressive, but they are so exuberant that they can easily knock grandpa or the kiddies on their keisters. This breed needs a strong-willed owner who can enforce primacy gently but firmly.

OWNER TRAITS

Special Perks: In general, the Weim is a great dog that tolerates children and loves its family. They also make excellent jogging partners—provided they don't get distracted by a biker, another runner, or a fleeing animal. Always remember that ownership of this breed is very much a two-way street. You will strive for obedience and good behavior. The typical Weim will take this into account, but also bring its own demands (face time, exercise, the latitude to claim any part of your home as its personal den) to the table. You and the dog will be happier if you approach these negotiations with a spirit of compromise—not to mention a sense of humor.

Bugs in the System: Subject to bloat, hip dysplasia, and immune system disorders.

If someone broke into my house, this dog would: Bark aggressively to ward him off. Unfortunately, they may also bark simply because they like the sound of their voice. For this reason (and others) they make lousy apartment dogs.

If you like the Weimaraner, check out: The slightly smaller vizsla.

*Weight: 25–30 pounds (11.3–13.5 kg). **Height:** 10–13 inches (25.4–33 cm). **Build:** A sturdy body on short legs. The Pembroke has no tail. The Cardigan is a little larger, with bigger ears. **Coat:** Short hair on the Pembroke, longer, softer hair on the Cardigan. Colors range from black and tan to fawn. **Brains:** Both corgi types are highly intelligent and easy to train. **Bladder Matters:** No house-training issues.*

The Incredible Origin: This breed is actually two, the Cardigan (named after the Welsh county of Cardiganshire) and the Pembroke. They are so similar that for a long time they were allowed to interbreed—until such nonsense was stopped in the early twentieth century. The Pembroke is slightly smaller and lacks a tail. The Cardigan has a tail and is larger and more substantial, with a more powerful muzzle and enormous, upright ears. The Pembroke tends to be more outgoing and vivacious, while the cardigan can be somewhat more laid-back and reserved. Though it's hard to imagine, this ungainly-looking animal was developed for (and is extremely good at) herding cattle. They do this by nipping at a cow's heels, then ducking to avoid being kicked. Today the Pembroke is by far the more popular of the two corgis, no doubt because Queen Elizabeth keeps a pack of them.

Trademark Traits: For a herding dog, the corgi can be an incredibly gentle, placid, and loving canine. Though somewhat independent (don't take them out unless they're on a leash), their open, friendly facial expression perfectly sums up their character.

Headaches and Hassles: If corgis had a support group, it might be called Dogs Who Love Children Too Much. Many corgis adore kids, but they may treat them like cattle and nip at their heels (a problem you'll need to address in training, whether you have children of your own or not). For this reason, this very kid-friendly dog often isn't suitable for families with very young children. Corgis also shed like mad in spring and fall and can be distrustful of strangers. The Cardigan can sometimes be *very* distrustful.

M

DOG TRAITS

WHO SHOULD GET THIS DOG?
Ideal for families with older children or single adults willing to give it the training and attention it needs. A country or suburban home is a must. The typical corgi is far too energetic and boisterous for apartment life.

OWNER TRAITS

Special Perks: It requires regular exercise, but this entails nothing more demanding than long walks and backyard romps in a fenced yard. The dog is clean and quiet in the house, and though it loves attention, it usually won't knock you over trying to get it.

Bugs in the System: Look out for spinal problems and a slew of eye issues. Though the massive ears of adult Cardigans usually stand erect, those of puppies fold. Taping is sometimes required to help them achieve their full, upright glory. Puppies must also be shown how to ascend and (more problematic, considering their body shape) descend stairs.

If someone broke into my house, this dog would: Corgis are outstanding watchdogs. They will keep tabs on your property, suspiciously eyeball strangers, and bark to raise the alarm if they spot something fishy.

If you like the Welsh corgi, check out: If low-slung dogs are your thing, take a look at the Dandie Dinmont terrier. For a grittier herding breed, consider the Australian cattle dog.

Weight: 15–22 pounds (6.8–9.9 kg). **Height:** 10–11 inches (25.4–27.9 cm). **Build:** Sturdy and stocky, with short legs. **Coat:** Thick, white, double coat, with wiry outer hair. **Brains:** Westies are highly intelligent and, given enough time, can learn very complex behaviors. They can sometimes, however, be a bit stubborn. **Bladder Matters:** No special house-training issues.

The Incredible Origin: In attitude, build, and coat, the "Westie" has much in common with other tiny terriers such as the cairn. The major difference is that, back in the day, a Scottish hunter decided to create a line of white terriers after mistaking one of his brownish cairns for a fox and shooting it. The happy result of that unhappy friendly fire incident has become one of the world's most popular show and companion dogs.

Trademark Traits: The Westie is not a lapdog. Instead of parking on top of its owner for hours on end, this independent breed would prefer to either (1) run around having fun, or (2) run around making trouble. Its choice will depend on how carefully it has been trained and socialized. Westies are very independent-minded—and very impressed with themselves.

Headaches and Hassles: The coat takes a lot of brushing and grooming, unless you want your Westie to turn into a mass of fur so unruly you won't be able to tell which end is which. Westies also like to dig, and they can become destructive if left alone too long or otherwise neglected. They are usually good with children, as long as the children are old enough to respect the dog's personal space. A poorly socialized dog may compulsively bark. It can have trouble (or make trouble) with other dogs and may give your cat some grief. They will bolt after squirrels and other small animals and therefore must always be leashed in public. Puppies can be particularly "busy," chewing, digging, and in general disrupting your day.

Special Perks: Westies are energetic, but they don't require endless walks. Some playtime in the evening and a few mad dashes around the yard will usually suffice. This breed's coat repels dirt and doesn't carry a pronounced "doggy" smell. They don't shed

DOG TRAITS

WHO SHOULD GET THIS DOG?

An individual or family willing to make a Westie part of their lives and give it the training and attention it craves. A good choice for active older people who can handle this dog's needs for exercise and attention.

OWNER TRAITS

all that much, and the hair they do drop is easy to spot. Plus, of course, you'll never mistake this dog for a fox when you're out hunting.

Bugs in the System: Subject to severe skin allergies, jaw problems, and hip-joint deterioration.

If someone broke into my house, this dog would: Bark loudly and at very great length. But then, Westies will bark loudly and at great length when *anyone* materializes at your front door.

If you like the Westie, check out: The West Highland's less-conspicuous ancestor, the cairn terrier. Or its all-black doppelgänger, the Scottish terrier.

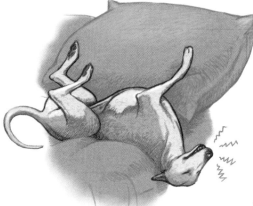

Weight: 19–22 *pounds (8.6–9.9 kg).* **Height:** *18–22 inches (45.7–55.9 cm).* **Build:** *Lithe, muscular, and graceful.* **Coat:** *Very short, in a wide color range.* **Brains:** *Above-average intelligence, though the sensitive whippet must be trained with kid gloves. Use the word "No!" one too many times, and you could break its spirit.* **Bladder Matters:** *No special house-training problems.*

The Incredible Origin: The whippet is a sort of economy-size greyhound, developed in the nineteenth century in northern England for rabbit hunting and, later, racing. It was allegedly crossed with terriers, but the modern versions seem to have lost any terrier-inspired aggressiveness. Today's enthusiasts hold rallies at which their whippets can race, but no betting is allowed.

Trademark Traits: This elegant little dog loves attention, but won't make a spectacle of itself trying to get it. It makes a good apartment dog, so long as it gets regular exercise and can occasionally run off-lead in a fenced area. Though capable of explosive speed, the whippet is also content to snuggle on the couch for hours on end.

Headaches and Hassles: It's hard to find something bad to say about the whippet, but here goes. They must always be kept on a leash in public, because if something piques their interest, they're gone—usually at around 40 mph (64.4 kph). Also, whippets will greet you enthusiastically when you come home. Of course all dogs do this, but whippets can act like you're coming home from a two-year hitch in the merchant marine. These dogs are going to sleep on your sofa or on whatever other furnishings catch their eye, so don't waste a lot of energy trying to prevent this behavior. Just cover its favorite chair with a blanket.

Special Perks: This dog is definitely not a barker. It is good with children (though it can be overwhelmed by too much boisterous activity), loves its family, and gets along with cats and other dogs. It also makes an excellent jogging partner, provided it is kept

DOG TRAITS

WHO SHOULD GET THIS DOG?

A family or individual willing to give it the exercise and love it needs. This breed is also good for apartment living, provided it gets to stretch its legs. It also makes both an excellent jogging partner and couch companion.

OWNER TRAITS

leashed. Though whippets can be very exuberant outdoors, in the house their favorite activity is piling up somewhere and snoozing for hours on end. Its coat needs very little attention, so you won't be making a ton of visits to the grooming salon.

Bugs in the System: Because it's so lean and its coat so short, the whippet suffers in the cold. Also, they need soft bedding to cushion their bony-looking frames. They are also, believe it or not, subject to sunburn. Inherited eye problems are another issue.

If someone broke into my house, this dog would: Bark, if the spirit moves them. But don't count on it. As a general rule, whippets are not very good watchdogs.

If you like the whippet, check out: The graceful and equally slight-looking Italian greyhound, or the sturdier, full-size greyhound.

Weight: 3–7 pounds (1.4–3.2 kg). **Height:** 7–9 inches (17.8–22.9 cm). **Build:** Tiny, yet athletic. **Coat:** Very long, very silky steel blue hair, with tan on the chest. **Brains:** Highly intelligent, though somewhat stubborn when it comes to obedience training. **Bladder Matters:** No special house-training problems.

The Incredible Origin: Developed in the nineteenth century to kill rats in British coal mines, the "Yorkie" was gradually downsized into a refined-looking (and absurdly small) companion dog. Today the Chihuahua is the only breed that's tinier than this diminutive rodent killer.

Trademark Traits: Yorkies only *look* like lapdogs. In fact, they are so energetic and feisty that your lap is often the last place they want to be. Utterly fearless and combative, these tiny canines buzz around the house like bugs. A typical Yorkie would enjoy, say, leaping onto your chair, climbing up to your face, sticking its tongue into your ear, and then vanishing before you can react.

Headaches and Hassles: Want a part-time job? Then try taking care of a Yorkie's glossy, long mane. Or you can simply get rid of it and give your dog a short (but still endearing) utility cut. Yorkies aren't particularly good with young children. Bother them or squeeze them too hard, and Junior may get a chomp on the arm for his trouble. Yorkies can get in trouble because they will attack dogs many times their size—dogs that, once they get over their amazement, could seriously hurt their smaller opponent. For this reason, a Yorkie can't be trusted off its leash in public. Their barking can get out of hand, particularly when they are left alone for long periods.

Special Perks: This is an ideal apartment dog (as long as the barking issue is addressed). Of course it needs exercise, but when the typical living room is as vast to them as a football field would be to us, getting a workout isn't a big deal.

DOG TRAITS

WHO SHOULD GET THIS DOG?

The Yorkie makes an excellent apartment dog. It's also good for families with older children, and seems to get on especially well with celebrities. Kirsten Dunst named hers Beauty; Britney Spears calls hers Baby; and tennis phenom Venus Williams has one named Pete, after Pete Sampras.

OWNER TRAITS

Bugs in the System: Eye problems, hip-joint disorders, and collapsing trachea, along with tooth decay and gum disease are typical Yorkie problems. Also, be wary of anyone offering to sell you a "teacup" Yorkie. These ridiculously tiny specimens can weigh anywhere between 1 and 2 pounds, which is just too small to be healthy. Such microscopic canines usually come with a raft of health problems and birth defects, and are so fragile they can be damaged or even killed by anything from a short fall to a missed meal. Responsible breeders feel so strongly about this that they won't even use the word "teacup" to describe undersized dogs.

If someone broke into my house, this dog would: Bark and bark and bark . . . and perhaps even attack. Yorkies are, for their size, excellent watchdogs.

If you like the Yorkie, check out: The cairn terrier—it has all the energy of a Yorkie in a slightly larger package. Or the Pomeranian, which has all the energy of a Yorkie in a slightly *fluffier* package.

Breed Organizations

The following groups can offer additional information about the dogs listed in this book, along with reputable channels (including responsible breeders and breed rescue services) through which puppies and adult dogs can be obtained. Many provide international, regional, and local contacts for breed clubs and rescue services.

GENERAL INFORMATION

The American Kennel Club
www.akc.org

American Society for the Prevention of Cruelty to Animals
www.aspca.org

Australian National Kennel Council
www.ankc.aust.com

The Humane Society of the United States
www.hsus.org

The Kennel Club (United Kingdom)
www.the-kennel-club.org.uk

Petfinder.com
A nationwide clearinghouse for the adoption of homeless pets.

BREED-SPECIFIC INFORMATION

Affenpinscher
Affenpinscher Club of America
www.affenpinscher.org

Afghan Hound
The Afghan Hound Club of America
www.clubs.akc.org/ahca

Airedale Terrier
The Airedale Terrier Club of America
www.airedale.org

Akita
The Akita Club of America
www.akitaclub.org
Japanese Akita Club of America
www.akita-inu.com

Alaskan Malamute
Alaskan Malamute Club of America
www.alaskanmalamute.org

American Foxhound
American Foxhound Club
www.americanfoxhoundclubinc.com

American Staffordshire Terrier
Staffordshire Terrier Club of America
www.amstaff.org

Australian Cattle Dog
Australian Cattle Dog Club of America
www.acdca.org

Basenji
Basenji Club of America
www.basenji.org

Basset Hound
Basset Hound Club of America
www.basset-bhca.org

Beagle
National Beagle Club of America
www.clubs.akc.org/NBC

Bearded Collie
Bearded Collie Club of America
www.beardie.net/bcca

Bedlington Terrier
The Bedlington Terrier Club of America
clubs.akc.org/btca

Bernese Mountain Dog
Bernese Mountain Dog Club of America
www.bmdca.org

Bichon Frise
The Bichon Frise Club of America
www.bichon.org

Bloodhound
The American Bloodhound Club
www.bloodhounds.org

Border Collie
The United States Border Collie Club
www.bordercollie.org/club.html

Border Terrier
The Border Terrier Club of America
www.clubs.akc.org/btcoa

Borzoi
Borzoi Club of America
www.borzoiclubofamerica.org/index.htm

Boston Terrier
Boston Terrier Club of America
www.bostonterrierclubofamerica.org

Bouvier des Flandres
The American Bouvier des Flandres Club
www.bouvier.org

Boxer
The American Boxer Club
www.americanboxerclub.org

Briard
Briard Club of America
www.briardclubofamerica.org

Brittany (Spaniel)
The American Brittany Club
www.clubs.akc.org/brit

Brussels Griffon
National Brussels Griffon Club
www.brussels-griffon.net

Bulldog (English)
The Bulldog Club of America
www.thebca.org

Bulldog (French)
The French Bulldog Club of America
www.frenchbulldogclub.org

Bullmastiff
The American Bullmastiff Association
www.clubs.akc.org/aba

Bull Terrier
Bull Terrier Club of America
www.btca.com

Cairn Terrier
Cairn Terrier Club of America
www.cairnterrier.org

Cavalier King Charles Spaniel
Cavalier King Charles Spaniel Club—USA
www.ckcsc.org

Chihuahua
The Chihuahua Club of America
www.chihuahuaclubofamerica.com

Chinese Crested
American Chinese Crested Club
www.crestedclub.org

Chinese Shar-Pei
Chinese Shar-Pei Club of America
www.cspca.com

Chow Chow
The Chow Chow Club
www.chowclub.org

Cocker Spaniel
American Spaniel Club
www.asc-cockerspaniel.org

Collie
Collie Club of America
www.collieclubofamerica.org

Dachshund
The Dachshund Club of America
www.dachshund-dca.org

Dalmatian
Dalmatian Club of America
www.thedca.org

Dandie Dinmont Terrier
Dandie Dinmont Terrier Club of America
www.clubs.akc.org/ddtca

Doberman Pinscher
Doberman Pinscher Club of America
www.dpca.org

Dogue de Bordeaux
Dogue de Bordeaux Society
www.ddbs.org

Fox Terrier
The American Fox Terrier Club
www.aftc.org

German Shepherd
German Shepherd Dog Club of America
www.gsdca.org

Golden Retriever
Golden Retriever Club of America
www.grca.org

Gordon Setter
Gordon Setter Club of America
www.gsca.org

Great Dane
Great Dane Club of America
www.gdca.org

Great Pyrenees
Great Pyrenees Club of America
clubs.akc.org/gpca

Greyhound
Greyhound Club of America
www.greyhoundclubofamerica.org

Harrier
Harrier Club of America
www.harrierclubofamerica.com

Irish Setter
Irish Setter Club of America
www.irishsetterclub.org

Irish Terrier
Irish Terrier Club of America
www.dogbiz.com/itca

Irish Wolfhound
Irish Wolfhound Club of America
www.iwclubofamerica.org

Italian Greyhound
Italian Greyhound Club of America
www.italiangreyhound.org

Jack Russell Terrier
Jack Russell Terrier Club of America
www.terrier.com
Parson Russell Terrier Association of America
www.jrtaa.org

Keeshond
The Keeshond Club of America
www.keeshond.org/home.html

Kerry Blue Terrier
United States Kerry Blue Terrier Club
www.uskbtc.com

Komondor
Komondor Club of America
clubs.akc.org/kca

Kuvasz
Kuvasz Club of America
www.kuvasz.com

Labrador Retriever
The Labrador Retriever Club
thelabradorclub.com

Lhasa Apso
The American Lhasa Apso Club
www.lhasaapso.org

Maltese
American Maltese Association
www.americanmaltese.org

Mastiff
Mastiff Club of America
www.mastiff.org

Mexican Hairless
Xoloitzcuintle Club USA
xolo.home.mindspring.com/xcusa.html

Miniature Pinscher
Miniature Pinscher Club of America
www.minpin.org

Neapolitan Mastiff
United States Neapolitan Mastiff Club
www.neapolitan.org

Newfoundland
Newfoundland Club of America
www.newfdogclub.org/index.html#Main

Norfolk/Norwich Terriers
The Norwich and Norfolk Terrier Club
clubs.akc.org/nntc

Old English Sheepdog
Old English Sheepdog Club of America
www.oldenglishsheepdogclubofamerica.org

Papillon
Papillon Club of America
www.papillonclub.org

Pekingese
Pekingese Club of America
www.geocities.com/Heartland/3843

Pomeranian
American Pomeranian Club
www.americanpomeranianclub.org

Poodle (Standard, Miniature, and Toy)
The Poodle Club of America
www.poodleclubofamerica.org

Pug
Pug Dog Club of America
www.pugs.org

Puli
Puli Club of America
www.puliclub.org

Rhodesian Ridgeback
The Rhodesian Ridgeback
Club of the United States
rrcus.org

Rottweiler
United States Rottweiler Club
www.usrcweb.org

Saint Bernard
Saint Bernard Club of America
www.saintbernardclub.org

Saluki
Saluki Club of America
www.salukiclub.org

Samoyed
Samoyed Club of America
www.samoyed.org/Samoyed_Club_of_America.html

Schipperke
Schipperke Club of America
www.schipperkeclub-usa.org

Schnauzer (Standard)
The Standard Schnauzer Club of America
www.standardschnauzer.org/staging/index.html

Schnauzer (Giant)
The Giant Schnauzer Club of America
www.giantschnauzerclubofamerica.com

Schnauzer (Miniature)
The American Miniature Schnauzer Club
amsc.us/index.html

Scottish Deerhound
Scottish Deerhound Club of America
www.deerhound.org/index.htm

Scottish Terrier
Scottish Terrier Club of America
clubs.akc.org/stca

Shetland Sheepdog (Sheltie)
American Shetland Sheepdog Association
www.assa.org

Shih Tzu
American Shih Tzu Club
www.shihtzu.org

Siberian Husky
Siberian Husky Club of America
www.shca.org/index.shtml

Spinone Italiano
Spinone Club of America
www.spinone.com/index.htm

Staffordshire Bull Terrier
Staffordshire Bull Terrier Club
clubs.akc.org/sbtci

Tibetan Spaniel
Tibetan Spaniel Club of America
www.tsca.ws

Vizsla
The Vizsla Club of America
clubs.akc.org/vizsla

Weimaraner
Weimaraner Club of America
weimclubamerica.org

Welsh Corgi
Cardigan Welsh Corgi Club of America
www.cardigancorgis.com

Pembroke Welsh Corgi Club of America
www.pembrokecorgi.org

West Highland White Terrier
West Highland White Terrier Club of America
www.westieclubamerica.com

Whippet
American Whippet Club
www.americanwhippetclub.net

Yorkshire Terrier
Yorkshire Terrier Club of America
www.ytca.org

Index By Category

Most U.S. breed guides list dogs under the seven major groups recognized by America's leading purebred association, the American Kennel Club. These are: herding dogs, hounds, nonsporting dogs, sporting dogs, terriers, toys, and working dogs (read more about these on page 16).

This book, however, lists breeds in alphabetical order, which makes it easy for the novice to find what he or she wants. But if you're interested in a particular group rather than a specific breed, the following type-by-type index will help.

At press time the Dogo Argentino, Dogue de Bordeaux, and Mexican hairless weren't recognized by the AKC, so you won't find them here. Also, the Jack Russell terrier is now officially referred to by the AKC as the Parson Russell terrier.

Index By Lifestyle

This index lists the breeds best suited to your lifestyle, ensuring a match made in doggy heaven.

ACKNOWLEDGMENTS

To assemble this book we sought guidance from breeders, dog associations and clubs, and, first and foremost, the selfless volunteers at regional, state, and local breed rescue services. These wonderful folks work tirelessly—and, often, thanklessly—to remove purebred canines from shelters or unsuitable living situations. They then find these animals new "forever homes" with people who will provide proper love and care.

Such efforts are emotionally and physically draining. Most rescue veterans can share stories of abuse, neglect, and abandonment that would wring tears from a statue. But none of this stops them from driving uncounted miles to retrieve surrendered dogs, and putting them up in their own homes, sometimes for months at a time. This made telephone interviews for this book something of an adventure, because the rescuers in question would usually have two or three examples of their breed at their feet, barking for attention. For instance, Charlotte Olsen of Guardian Angel Basset Rescue gamely spent half an hour on the phone while her pack of bassets bayed in the background. In spite of the disruption, she imparted great wisdom without so much as a single "Huh?" or "What was I saying?" For instance, we learned that Olsen's favorite breed is adept at "counter surfing"—quickly relieving kitchen counters of any unattended foodstuffs, ranging from stray crumbs to Thanksgiving turkeys.

With similar distractions, Paula Harshberger, coordinator and advisory director of BRAT (Basenji Rescue & Transport, Inc.), shared the unsettling fact that while basenjis don't bark, they can utter a hideous scream. A scream that she described, in an impossible-to-improve-upon turn of phrase, as "like a baby being murdered."

Most of these hardworking people were more than willing to "badmouth" the breeds they love, in hopes that some potential owners—the sorts of people who aren't right for the dog—will think twice before acquiring one. To do that, they freely told us that Neapolitan mastiffs can "sulk," that Border collies can "easily learn things that you don't want them to learn," that some Great Danes "show signs of attention deficit disorder," and that Brittanys "are quite capable of acting dumb."

Saying such things doesn't put dogs in the best possible light, but it's done for the best possible reason—to make sure that the people who consider adopting them know, really know, what they're getting into. And if their honest assessments and wry observations keep more dogs from landing in the wrong hands, this book will be worth its weight in gold.